Collins

Japanese

Phrasebook
and Dictionary

D0456590

Japanese Phrasebook and
Dictionary

Other languages in the
Collins Phrasebook and Dictionary
series:
French, German, Greek, Italian,
Mandarin, Polish, Portuguese,
Spanish, Turkish.

HarperCollins Publishers
Westerhill Road, Bishopbriggs,
Glasgow G64 2QT

www.collinslanguage.com

First published 2004
This edition published 2008

Reprint 10 9 8 7 6 5 4 3 2 1 0

© HarperCollinsPublishers 2004,
2008

ISBN 978-0-00-726458-2

All rights reserved.

Typeset by Davidson Pre-Press
Graphics Ltd, Glasgow

Printed in Malaysia by Imago

Contents

Your *Collins Japanese Phrasebook and Dictionary* is a handy, quick-reference guide that will help make the most of your stay abroad. Its clear layout will save valuable time when you need that crucial word or phrase. Download free all the essential words and phrases you need to get by from www.collinslanguage.com/talk60. These hour long audio files are ideal for practising listening comprehension and pronunciation. The main sections in this book are:

Everyday Japan - photoguide
Packed full of photos, this section allows you to see all the practical visual information that will help with using cash machines, driving on motorways, reading signs, etc.

Phrases
Practical topics are arranged thematically with an opening section, Key talk containing vital phrases that should stand you in good stead in most situations. Phrases are short, useful and each one has a pronunciation guide so that there is no problem saying them.

Eating out
This section contains phrases for ordering food and drink (and special requirements) plus a photoguide showing different places to eat, menus and practical information to help choose the best options. The menu reader allows you to work out what to choose.

Grammar
There is a short Grammar section explaining how the language works.

Dictionary
And finally, the practical English-Japanese Dictionary means that you won't be stuck for words.

So, just flick through the pages to find the information you need and listen to the free audio download to improve your pronunciation.

Useful websites

Accommodation
www.abouthotel.com
www.jnto.go.jp

Currency Converter
www.x-rates.com

Driving
www.jaf.or.jp/e/index_e.htm
(Japan Automobile Federation
– JAF)

Facts
www.cia.gov/library/publications
/the-world-factbook/index.html
(country profile of Japan)

Food
www.bento.com
(a guide to Japanese cuisine
and eating out in Tokyo)

Foreign Office Advice
www.fco.gov.uk/travel
www.dfat.gov.au (Australia)
www.voyage.gc.ca (Canada)

Health advice
www.dh.gov.uk/travellers
www.thetraveldoctor.com
www.smartraveller.gov.au
(Australia)
www.phac-aspc.gc.ca (Canada)

Internet Cafés
www.cybercafes.com

Outdoor Activities
www.outdoorjapan.com
(information about hiking,
onsen – hot springs, camping,
golf, etc)

Passport Office
www.ukpa.gov.uk
www.passports.gov.au (Australia)
www.pptc.gc.ca (Canada)

Sightseeing
www.jnto.go.jp (Japan National
Tourist Organization)
www.japan-guide.com
(guide to Japan)
www.hatobus.com (coach
sightseeing tours of Tokyo)
www.pref.nara.jp
(website to Nara prefecture)

Transport
www.jnto.go.jp/eng/GA
(information on getting around
Japan)
www.japanrailpass.net
(information on Japan Rail
Pass)
www.narita-airport.jp/en/
(information on Narita
International airport)

Weather
www.bbc.co.uk/weather

Although Japanese has an extremely complicated writing system, it is a grammatically simple language that is very easy to pronounce. Provided you follow a few set rules and learn a few set phrases, you will be surprised at how far you can get by.

The basic unit of speech is the syllable, not the letter. Every syllable is pronounced quite evenly and rather flatly, and stress is much more subtle. For example, Paris is pronounced **Pa**ris in English and pa**ree** in French, while in Japanese it is **Pa-ree** – with equal stress on both syllables.

Japanese has relatively few sounds. Vowels have only one sound (rather like Italian):

Vowels

a is pronounced as in b**a**th
e is pronounced as in l**e**t
i is pronounced as in pol**i**ce
o is pronounced as in g**o**t
u is pronounced as in p**u**t

Vowel combinations

Japanese vowels differ from English ones in that they do not change their sounds when combined with other vowels. To pronounce the **kai** of **kaizen**, for example, you simply say **ka** (as in '**ca**rt') and **i** (as in 'b**i**t') without a pause.

ai is pronounced as in Th**ai**land
ae is pronounced as if it were hyphenated **a-eh**
ei is pronounced as in n**ei**gh

A bar on top of a vowel indicates that it is twice as long, e.g. in the case of **Kyōto** the first **o** is double the length of the second one. You should take care to pronounce these long vowels clearly otherwise the meaning of the word may change.

Consonants (**b**, **c**, **s**, **t**, etc) are close to their English equivalents, but note the following:

g is always hard, as in **golf**, never as in **Germany**
y is always pronounced as in **young**, never as in **cry**

Double consonants, like the double 't' in **kitte**, are pronounced by leaving a very slight pause before the consonant, then expressing it very clearly, as if the word had two halves. For example: **kite** has the same stress as the English 'kitty', but **kitte** sounds more like 'kids' day'.

Since Japanese lacks the consonants **l** and **v**, foreign loanwords with these letters are pronounced with **r** and **b**, respectively. Thus, the three English words 'love', 'lab' and 'rub', all become indistinguishable as **ra-bu** in Japanese.

Japanese also lacks the **si** sound (as in 'to sit'), and **shi** is used instead, with often embarrassing results, e.g. 'babysitter' becomes **be-bi-shi-ttā**! Other English sounds that do not exist in Japanese are **hu** (as in 'hook'; **fu** is used instead), **th** (as in 'thin'; **sh** is used instead) and **ti** (as in 'tin'; **chi** is used instead).

Remember to pronounce each syllable clearly and separately. Foreign loanwords (including your own name) are 'Japanized' by making each syllable end in a vowel. Thus, Mr Smith becomes **Mi-su-tā Su-mi-su**, Grand Hotel becomes **Gu-ra-n-do Ho-te-ru** and taxi becomes **ta-ku-shī**. However u and i are pronounced very faintly, so **Mi-su-tā** becomes **mista** and **gu-ra-n-do** becomes **grando**. The only exception is when a word ends with the letter **n**, like **supāman** 'Superman'. If you don't know the Japanese for a word, Japanizing the English equivalent may well work.

You should also remember that Japanese does not have a silent e at the end of a word such as in the English 'to take'. If 'take' is read as the Japanese word **take** (bamboo), it should be pronounced tah-keh. Similarly with **sake** (rice wine), pronounced sah-keh, or **ike** (pond), pronounced eeh-keh, etc.

HOKKAIDŌ

Sapporo

JAPAN SEA

Morioka

Sendai

Nīgata

HONSHŪ

Tōkyō

Mt. Fuji

Nagoya

Kyōto

Kōbe

Ōsaka

Hiroshima

Fukuoka

SHIKOKU

KYŪSHŪ

Nagasaki

PACIFIC OCEAN

Everyday photoguide

Everyday Japan

Japanese Writing Written either horizontally or vertically. Traditionally from top to bottom, starting at the right-hand top corner of the page. With modernization, it also became written horizontally from left to right.

Open 24 Hours
Shops open from 10am–8pm. Many are open seven days a week (including public holidays, except for New Year). Some are closed one day per week (**Teikyūbi**).

Parking Entrance Japanese script is based on Chinese-derived characters called **kanji**.

Emergency Exit Pictograms are often used in Japan.

Open   Closed

In   Out

Prices are generally written with western numbers as are weights and time. Japan is fully metric.

円

Symbol for **yen**. It is pronounced en not yen. The international symbol is ¥.

Logo for post office cash machine.

Money Most ATMs in Japan do not accept cards of non-Japanese banks. Many only work during banking hours although some work until 6 or 7pm, and at weekends but it would not be wise to rely on obtaining cash from them. In larger cities, some ATMs accept overseas bank cards, usually via the Cirrus system. It is possible to get cash advances on major credit cards through the bigger Japanese banks, though service varies from branch to branch.

Thousands of **yen** are separated by a comma. Japanese banknotes are of relatively large denominations, ¥1,000, ¥2,000, ¥5,000 and ¥10,000. Coins are ¥1 (aluminium), ¥5 (brass with hole in middle), ¥10 (brass), ¥50 (nickel with hole in middle), ¥100 and ¥500.

Bank Hours Banks are open 9am–3pm, Monday to Friday and closed at weekends and on public holidays. Citibank, which has branches in all the big cities, is most orientated to dealing with foreigners. You can change money easily at Narita Airport. Travellers' cheques can be cashed at most major banks, for a fee, but some only accept them if they are in US dollars.

There are automatic paying machines for tickets, parking, etc. You can use cash with these. Some, though not many, accept major international credit cards.

A 5% consumption tax (equivalent to VAT) is added to prices (except for a number of everyday items such as stamps and newspapers). So for a ¥1000 item you will be asked to pay ¥1050. To avoid breaking into another note, have a pocketful of small change to pay the tax. There is no tipping in Japan – in restaurants there is a service charge (usually 10%) plus the consumption charge.

Japan has a population of approximately 127 million and cities can become awfully crowded – especially on public transport during the rush hour or at shopping centres at weekends. Space is a premium in Japan and high prices charged in some places (like traditional coffee shops) reflect this. The high charge isn't so much for the drink but for the space rented out. You can stay for as long as you like.

Traditional Japanese buildings were made of wood. The more traditional an eating or drinking establishment, the more often wood is used in its decor.

Streets are kept immaculately clean. There is no litter and there are recycling bins outside shops.

Umbrella Stands
During the rainy season, you will need an umbrella for the frequent showers.

No Smoking
Smoking remains widespread in Japan. It is forbidden on all trains, buses and planes. It is more loosely prohibited in restaurants, some of which have 'no smoking' sections of varying effectiveness but it is generally permitted in smaller establishments, bars, game centres etc.

Karaoke booths are extremely popular and you find that time can become distorted in them. What feels like an hour to you is probably more likely to be five hours! If you are invited to do a turn at the microphone, forget any inhibitions and enjoy yourself.

To Let Telephone numbers are usually written in western numerals.

Cigarette Vending

Food Display
Many eating establishments have a display of plates with plastic food on them to show you what they offer.

Vending Machines Jidōhanbaīki (shortened to **jihanki**) is the word for vending machine. You can get practically anything from them: hot tea and coffee in a tin, cold tea, cold beer, tights, knickers, etc. Hot drinks will be identified with red buttons, cold with blue. Machines selling alcohol shut down at night and are becoming rare.

Water Tap water is safe to drink all over Japan. However in the hot, muggy summer, it is worth carrying a small bottle of mineral water around with you.

Lottery Logo

押

Push

引

Pull

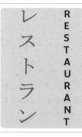

Reading Japanese Katakana is the angular script used for words of foreign origin known as 'loanwords'. It is worth trying to learn this as well as some **kanji** (Chinese-derived characters). There are 46 basic syllables in both **hiragana** and **katakana**. **Hiragana** is used with **kanji** for ordinary writing to show verb endings, etc.

Signs To Local Places Direction signs throughout Japan are almost always in English as well as Japanese.

Fire Hydrant Many signs are located high above the street.

Pedestrian Area Many signs are internationally recognizable.

Police The gold badge indicates a police station.

Street Sign Locator

Street Name Finding addresses in Japan can be quite complicated, even for Japanese people.

5-chome = block 5
4 = number 4

Streets in Japanese cities are often narrow and more suited to bikes and small cars. You have to pay for your parking space, it doesn't often come with your dwelling. Toll roads are also very expensive. Outside main cities there is not a great deal of traffic.

Cycle Lane These are clearly marked. Bicycles approach swiftly and silently, so it pays to be alert

Bicycles Bikes are used routinely in Japan. There are bike lanes on pavements which you should look out for.

Do Not Abandon Bike Sign

Bike Parking There is ample parking for bikes in Japanese cities. Many bikes have footrests on the back for a passenger to stand on. You can hire bikes from youth hostels and cycling terminals.

Parking There is no roadside parking in cities except in designated areas. There are car parks, parking meters and multistorey car parks.

Space-saving Japanese parking.

Parking Meter Display showing time remaining.

Spaces Look out for red script if the car park is full.

Driving is on the left and speeds are in kilometres per hour. Take care on windy roads, some Japanese drivers tend to cut corners and you should use your car horn on approaching sharp bends.

Petrol Stations These are not self-service. A number of personnel will tend to your needs. You need to ask for 'gasoline' – the word 'petrol' will not be understood.

A 24-hour coin-operated parking lot. The barrier in front of the car prevents it from leaving until the fee is paid at the machine. This is the cheapest way to park overnight.

Timetables

		Days
月曜	**getsu-yōbi**	Monday
火曜	**ka-yōbi**	Tuesday
水曜	**sui-yōbi**	Wednesday
木曜	**moku-yōbi**	Thursday
金曜	**kin-yōbi**	Friday
土曜	**do-yōbi**	Saturday
日曜	**nichi-yōbi**	Sunday

2008年5月現在

Dates You see western numbers mixed with **kanji**. Dates are written with the year first, then the month and then the day.

24時まで営業

Open Till Midnight

		Months
一月	**ichi-gats**	January
二月	**ni-gats**	February
三月	**san-gats**	March
四月	**shi-gats**	April
五月	**go-gats**	May
六月	**roku-gats**	June
七月	**shichi-gats**	July
八月	**hachi-gats**	August
九月	**ku-gats**	September
十月	**jū-gats**	October
十一月	**jū-ichi-gats**	November
十二月	**jū-ni-gats**	December

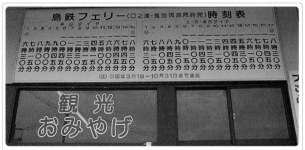

3	13	20	33	37
3	13	20	33	37
3	13	20	26	33
3	13	20	26	30
3	13	20	26	30
3	10	13	20	26
10	13	20	33	43
16	23	33	40	50
18	26	33		
0	7	46		

Departures

11:16	特急 L.Ltd.	成田エクスプレス14号 Narita Express No.14	池袋・大宮 Ikebukuro/Ōfuna	品川 Shinagawa
11:47	快速 Rapid		逗子 Zushi	土休日 Saturdays...
12:16	特急 L.Ltd.	成田エクスプレス16号 Narita Express No.16	池袋・横浜 Ikebukuro/Yokohama	品川 Shinagawa
13:03	快速 Rapid		逗子 Zushi	Commute...
13:16	特急 L.Ltd.	成田エクスプレス18号 Narita Express No.18	池袋・大宮 Ikebukuro/Ōfuna	品川 Shinagawa
13:47	快速 Rapid		逗子 Zushi	
14:15	特急 L.Ltd.	成田エクスプレス20号 Narita Express No.20	新宿 Shinjuku	
14:45	特急 L.Ltd.	成田エクスプレス22号 Narita Express No.22	横浜 Yokohama	品川 伊 Shinagawa
15:02	快速 Rapid		逗子 Zushi	

Times

Reading The Timetable The different colours represent different kinds of trains. The word for timetable is **jikoku-hyō**.

Ferry Timetable Notice that the times on this ferry timetable are written in Japanese rather than western numerals. They are also written vertically. The further you go off the beaten track, the less westernization you find.

Getting around

Japan National Tourist Organization
The JNTO website is full of practical
information and useful links. You should
visit it before your trip to Japan –
www.jnto.go.jp. There are many **TIC**
offices all over Japan. They provide maps
and brochures in English.

Tourist
Information
Center (TIC)

Right

Left

Exit

西 West　中 Centre　東 East

北 North

南 South

Entrance

Bus and Taxi Stop Guide Taxis are efficient, clean, safe and no more expensive than in most major world cities, especially when you consider that there is no tipping. Many now take major credit cards. Taxis are more often to be found late at night outside main hotels. Heavy traffic in cities means that the subway or train are often better options.

The driver automatically opens the doors and boot, so stand well back. There's a surcharge between 11pm and 5am.

Bus When you board this type of bus you get a ticket with a number. As the bus continues along its route, the fareboard changes. You pay the appropriate fee at your destination for your number ticket. Have someone write down your destination so that you can recognize it on the board.

Taxi Stand You can find taxi stances at stations and hotels. They can also be hailed in the street (provided the red light is illuminated).

Entrance To Subway The metro system in Japan is known as the subway. Most lines link with the Japanese overground network.

The different lines are colour-coded.

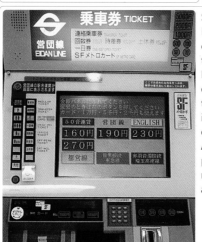

Subway Ticket Machine You can choose English from the touch screen. Note the pictograms on the extreme left of the photo, these indicate the different options available. Also shown are pictograms of the notes and coins accepted.

Subway lines are colour-coded. The subway is the quickest, easiest and cheapest way of getting around large cities. Avoid the rush hours if you can.

Subway Entrances and Exits

The different subway exits are numbered and marked on the map with English translations beneath. Some stations have many levels and exits. The word for platform sounds like 'home'.

Subway Entrance

Note the entrance number in the right corner and different colour-coded lines for this station.

Japanese Railway You can exchange the Japan Rail Pass voucher at the JR office at Narita Airport and use it on the Narita Express into Tokyo city centre. The Japan Rail Pass has to be purchased before you arrive in Japan. Visit **www.japanrailpass.net** for details.

Highway Buses are an economical alternative to trains and planes. They connect all major and most minor cities in Japan, and many run through the night. Destinations are also posted in English.

Station Kiosk You can get all the usual things: food, drink, books, gifts and travel goods.

Stations on many city lines are numbered, and boards like this show not only where you are, but the previous and next stations too.

Bullet Train – Shinkansen Japanese trains are famous for sticking to timetables. Even a 2-minute delay is practically unheard of. Trains stop for a short time to let people on or off, so you have to move smartly.

Luggage Locker Coin-operated luggage lockers tend to be quite small. Even on the trains, space for luggage is quite restricted. Travel as light as you can.

Destination Boards in subway and railway stations announce the next train, usually in English also. Here, the current location of the train is shown in the lower part.

Pictograms show all the facilities available.

Shopping

Streets can get very crowded, especially at weekends. Try and choose a quiet time to shop. All the branded chains can be found in the cities. Tokyo is a good place to buy trainers, as the fashion cycle is so fast that the major brands promote a vast array of styles and colours not found elsewhere (often with 50% discount).

Bookshop They can be open quite late but rarely stock anything in English. English language newspapers can be bought at railway stations, large hotels and some convenience stores.

Convenience Store Most areas have a convenience store (**conbeni**) open 24 hours selling all manner of necessities.

Photobooth You must always carry personal identification (passport, identity card) with you.

Traditional hardware stores like this are still very common selling high quality tools, scissors and other handy items.

Shopping malls usually have a variety of eating places which are displayed photographically. The letter 'F' stands for floor. Most eating places have a board showing photos of the meals they offer.

Shoe Shop
Imported shoes are expensive in Japan due to import tax. However, Japanese-made shoes are good value. Shoes are very popular with the Japanese.

Liquor Store You have to be over twenty to buy alcohol in Japan. And over twenty to smoke.

Pharmacy The green cross sign is used. Japanese medicines are of high quality but relatively expensive.

Bottled Water
Tap water in Japan is fine to drink, but many people prefer mineral water. Sparkling water is not as common as still water.

Milk is called **miruku** or **gyūnyū**, semi-skimmed milk is **teishibō gyūnyū** and skimmed milk is **mushibō gyūnyū**. Soya milk is **tōnyū**. When you order tea or coffee in a cafe you are generally given a small jug of cream.

Today's Special Offer

Sashimi Display Sashimi is raw fish. The largest size would be for a family of 3 or 4. This is a dish that would not generally be prepared at home.

Bread The word for bread is **pan**.

Fruit and vegetables In supermarkets nearly everything is shrinkwrapped and you need only choose what you want and take it to the checkout.

Fish Display
Fish is sold in cuts, or as cleaned whole fish. It is priced by weight and cut.

Checkout Checkouts operate as at home. They provide free plastic bags. Many supermarkets operate a loyalty-card system and you may be asked if you have one. Outside cities shops may not have a facility for taking credit cards.

Somewhere to stay

Ryokan Staying in a traditional Japanese inn (**ryokan**) allows you to experience Japanese traditional ways. The price usually includes dinner and breakfast. A **minshuku** is a cheaper version of the **ryokan**, usually bigger and only in main tourist resorts.

Ryokan provide towels, toiletries and nightwear in the form of a **yukata** (see left) – a cotton gown that can be worn indoors and should be worn in the hotel once you are checked in. Both men and women wear them.

A maid arranges your bath, serves dinner in your room and lays out the futon for you to sleep on.

You are served your meals in your room. Take care not to wear shoes on the **tatami** matting.

Hotel Rates Japan offers a wide range of accommodation.

Capsule Hotel These hotels comprise tiny self-contained cubicles stacked on top of each other, with communal washing facilities and vending machines for food, drink and toiletries.

Love Hotel 'Love hotels' are not as sleazy as they sound – they are often luxurious, clean and rooms often have great decor. They offer couples total discretion and privacy for 2-hour periods during the day. They're also used by Japanese married couples to get some privacy. Overnight stays (generally after 10pm and checking out before 10am) get cheaper rates.

Toilets and baths

Toilets There is a great deal of delicacy associated with using the toilet. On trains there are western-style sit-on toilets and Japanese crouch over toilets. Elsewhere mostly western predominate. In a public toilet there is no hand towel or blow-dryer, so carry a little face cloth (**hankachi**) with you. The bathroom and toilet are always kept separate, and toilet slippers will be provided, leave your own outside the door. Never leave smells in the toilet in a private house, use the deodorant provided. Check before using that you can see the toilet handle. If there is none, crouch in front and feel over the body of the toilet. You will find a little secret drawer, like on a CD player. Be careful not to get sprayed by the bidet function! To use a Japanese-style toilet, you squat and face the 'windscreen' end. Check you can squat and make sure you don't have loose change in your back pocket!

Standard pictograms are used to indicate men's, ladies' and disabled toilets.

Toilets Western-style toilets are very advanced with warm seats and wash and blow-dry options. A warmed-seat toilet is called a **Warmlet**. The **Washlet** has a button called 'Bidet' which does a front wash. The **Derriere** button does a back wash. There will also be a drying button.

Disabled Toilet
Sign showing opening hours.

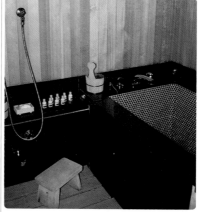

Tissue Vending Machine Always carry tissues with you as they are often not available in public toilets.

Japanese Bath You must shower thoroughly at the shower stool before entering a traditional Japanese bath (or **onsen** – hot spring, or **sento** – public bath). **Onsen** and **sento** have large shared pools so you need to be clean before entering. There will be a changing room where you put your clothes into a basket and wrap a cotton towel around you. Take a larger towel with you for drying (or hire one at the desk). The wash area has individual tap, bowls and stool areas. You soap and rinse all over, pouring or scooping the water from the bowl. Then make sure that you empty your bowl and sluice it down along with the shower utensils and stool before entering the bath or hot spring. On no account take soap into the **onsen** or **sento**.

Japanese life

Always remove shoes when entering someone's home or before sitting on **tatami** matting.

Onsen You should try to experience a hot spring during your visit. The website **www.outdoor.japan.com** has details and information. If you are a westerner and sharing with Japanese folk, be prepared to feel like a giant. Watching the sunset from an outdoor pool is a must.

Japan has 2 major religions – **shintō** and buddhism. This gate called **torii** is a feature of every **shintō** shrine.

This is a **tokonoma** which is an alcove for decorative art.

Much of Japan is still built in wood. Though some wooden buildings have been lost to redevelopment.

This wayside Buddha (**Jizo**) is carefully maintained by people from its neighbourhood.

Summer in Japan can be very humid with frequent showers. The cherry blossom is out from early to late April (earlier, the further south you are). Autumn is when the maple leaves turn crimson and the days are clear and cool. Major national holidays are Golden week (late April/early May) and **Obon** (mid-August).

These boxes contain branches from the tree which Japanese people take to the cemeteries.

Keeping in touch

Postboxes are red. If there are 2 slits, one is for regular mail, the other for express.

Public Phone
This phone box features a green phone that takes ten-yen and hundred-yen coins as well as phone cards. It does not make international calls as there is no 'international' plaque.

Letters can be addressed in **romaji** (western letters) but write clearly and in capitals. The city is written first and the addressee last. The small printed boxes on envelopes and postcards are for the post or zip code **yūbin bangō**.

You can get phonecards for domestic and international use. Green-coloured phones take coins and cards. Green and gold phones can be used to make international calls also usually indicated on a plaque on the phone.

international dialling codes	
Japan	00 81
US/Canada	00 1
UK	00 44
Australia	00 61

You can hire mobile phones at Narita and Kansai Airports, as your own phone won't work. Phone numbers are written in western numerals. 0120 is a freephone number.

Key talk

Key talk

• English is learnt at school in Japan, but mostly reading and translating, not so much speaking.
• There are levels of politeness in Japanese and although it would be impossible for a foreigner to be aware of them all, care should be taken to act politely and not be too loud.
• **Sumimasen** is an all-purpose word. You can use it to attract someone's attention before making a request. You can use it in a crowded train to get past people. It also means 'sorry'!

hello/ good afternoon	こんにちわ kon-nichi wa
goodbye	さようなら sayōnara
bye	バイバイ bai-bai
good morning	おはようございます ohayō gozaimass
good evening	こんばんわ konban wa
good night	おやすみなさい oyasumi nasai
good morning, Mrs Nakamura (polite)	中村さん、おはようございます Nakamura-san, ohayō gozaimass
please	どうぞ dōzo

thank you	ありがとう
	arigatō
thanks very much	どうもありがとう
	domo arigatō
yes	はい
	hai
no	いいえ
	ī-e
yes please	はいお願いします
	hai onegai shimass
no thank you	結構です
	kekkō dess
excuse me!/sorry!	すみません!
	sumimasen!
I'm very sorry	申し訳ありません
	mōshiwake arimasen

- US English is more widely understood in Japan. Remember to use 'subway' rather than underground and 'gasoline' rather than petrol, if you find you are not being understood.
- Even if you don't know the Japanese word for something, try Japanizing the English word and adding **kudasai** (please).
- Japanese is based on syllables so card = **kādo**, beer = **bīru**, tour = **tsuā** (see Pronouncing Japanese, p6).

Mr.../Mrs.../Ms...	...さん
	...-san
are you Mrs Nakamura?	中村さんですか
	Nakamura-san dess ka?
my name is Caroline Smart	私はキャロライン　スマートです
	watashi wa Caroline Smart dess
do you understand?	わかりますか
	wakarimass ka?

I don't understand	わかりません
	wakarimasen
do you speak English?	英語を話せますか
	eigo o hanasemass ka?
I don't speak Japanese	私は日本語を話せません
	watashi wa nihongo o hanasemasen
excuse me	すみません
	sumimasen
please help me	手伝ってください
	tetsudatte kudasai
what is this?	これはなんですか
	kore wa nan dess ka?
this one please	これを下さい
	kore o kudasai
that one please	それを下さい
	sore o kudasai

- Japanese tend not to use assertive words like 'yes' and 'no'.
- **ī-e** (meaning 'no') is best avoided. Looking doubtful works well.
- If a Japanese is saying 'no', they are more likely to let their reply tail off and not finish the sentence. This conveys 'no' by indicating that there is some difficulty with what you have asked.

...please	...を下さい
	...o kudasai
a coffee please	コーヒーを下さい
	kōhī o kudasai
a coca cola please	コカコーラを下さい
	koka-kora o kudasai
I would like.../ please can I have...	...お願いします
	...onegai shimass
I would like a glass	グラスお願いします
	gurass onegai shimass

I would like a fork	フォークお願いします
	fōku onegai shimass
do you have...?	…はありますか
	…wa arimass ka?
do you have a map?	地図はありますか
	chizu wa arimass ka?
do you have stamps?	切手はありますか
	kitte ga arimass ka?
do you have postcards?	ポストカードはありますか
	postokādo wa arimass ka?
do you have milk?	牛乳はありますか
	miruku wa arimass ka?

• Japanese people who speak English are likely to come up to a foreigner and offer help if they see them looking lost.
• Have cards made with your name and address. They don't need to be elaborate – ones you print yourself and cut up are fine.
• When you receive a business card, examine it carefully and try to pronounce the name. Then make sure you are seen putting it carefully into your wallet.

how much is/ are...?	…はいくらですか
	…wa ikura dess ka?
how much is that?	それはいくらですか
	sore wa ikura dess ka?
how much are the bananas?	バナナはいくらですか
	banana wa ikura dess ka?
how much is the map?	地図はいくらですか
	chizu wa ikura dess ka?
how much is the camera?	カメラはいくらですか
	kamera wa ikura dess ka?
how much is the entrance fee?	入場料はいくらですか
	nyū-jō-ryō wa ikura dess ka?

where is/are...?	...はどこですか
	...wa doko dess ka?
where is the bank?	銀行はどこですか
	ginkō wa doko dess ka?
where is the tourist office?	旅行案内所はどこですか
	ryokō annai-jo wa doko dess ka?
where is the toilet?	トイレはどこですか
	toire wa doko dess ka?
where is the hotel?	ホテルはどこですか
	hoteru wa doko dess ka?
the nearest...	一番近い...
	ichiban chikai...
where is the nearest...?	一番近い　はどこですか
	ichiban chikai ... wa doko dess ka?

- You should address someone you meet by their surname followed by **-san** (for both men and women). So Mrs Junko Hara would be **Hara-san** to most people she knows. If you get on very well, she will ask you to call her Junko and you would call her **Junko-san**. If you miss off the **-san** or use the first name without express permission, you will cause shock!
- You're more likely to be addressed by your first name followed by **-san**, e.g. **Carol-san**, because this is how you are generally known.

where is the nearest pharmacy?	一番近い薬局はどこですか
	ichiban chikai yakkyok wa doko dess ka?
where is the nearest hotel?	一番近いホテルはどこですか
	ichiban chikai hoteru wa doko dess ka?
where is the nearest police box?	一番近い交番はどこですか
	ichiban chikai kōban wa doko dess ka?
is it...?	...ですか
	...dess ka?

is it far?	遠いですか
	tōi dess ka?
is it nearby?	近いですか
	chikai dess ka?
is/are there...?	...はありますか
	...wa arimass ka?
is there a ryokan?	旅館はありますか
	ryokan wa arimass ka?
is there a hot spring?	温泉はありますか
	onsen wa arimass ka?
there is/are no...	...はありません
	...wa arimasen
there are no towels	タオルはありません
	taoru wa arimasen

• You shouldn't eat or drink while walking along the street or on public transport. You will find the streets very clean and there are numerous recycling bins outside shops.
• Japan is a very safe country and there is very little chance of being robbed or mugged.
• Guests are normally entertained in restaurants. If you are a business visitor, you will be taken out and not invited to a home. However, a tourist might be invited to a Japanese home.

I need...	...をお願いします
	...o onegai shimass
I need a receipt	レシートをお願いします
	reshīto o onegai shimass
I need to phone	電話をかけたいです
	denwa o kaketai dess
I need a taxi	タクシーを呼んでください
	takshī o yonde kudasai
may I/we...?	...してもいいですか
	...shtemo ī dess ka?

may I drive?	運転してもいいですか
	unten shtemo ī dess ka?
where can I buy a camera?	カメラはどこで買えますか
	kamera wa doko de kaemass ka?
where can I buy a mobile phone?	携帯電話はどこで買えますか
	keitai denwa wa doko de kaemass ka?
how do I work this?	どのように使えばいいですか
	dono yō ni tsukaeba ī dess ka?
what's this called in Japanese?	これは日本語で何と言いますか
	kore wa nihongo de nan to īmass ka?

• Always make sure you have no holes in your socks/tights, as you may have to take off your shoes unexpectedly.
• Always remove shoes when entering someone's home or before stepping onto **tatami** matting. Some Japanese restaurants have **tatami** matting and you will have to remove your shoes.
• Summers are very humid in most of Japan, so carry some water, a small towel and a fan with you.

when?	いつ
	itsu?
at what time?	何時に
	nan-ji ni?
when does the train leave?	電車は何時に出ますか
	densha wa nan-ji ni demass ka?
when is check-out time?	チェックアウトは何時ですか
	chekk-auto wa nan-ji dess ka?
when do you open?	いつ開きますか
	itsu akimass ka?
when do you close?	いつ閉まりますか
	itsu shimarimass ka?
this morning	今朝
	kesa

this afternoon	午後
	gogo
this evening	今夜
	konya
today	今日
	kyō
tomorrow	明日
	ashta
yesterday	昨日
	kinō
now	今
	ima
later	あとで
	ato de

- Personal space is important to Japanese people – don't sit or stand too close to them when talking.
- You should speak softly. Japanese don't like loud voices.
- When blowing your nose in public, be as quiet and unobtrusive as possible. Use paper tissues, as Japanese use handkerchiefs to wipe hands and foreheads.
- You shouldn't point at people with your index finger – use your whole hand, palm upwards in a flowing motion.

I'm...	私は … です
	watashi wa … dess
British	イギリス人
	igiriss-jin
Australian	オーストラリア人
	ōstoraria-jin
American	アメリカ人
	amerika-jin
my name is Jane Shaw	私はジェーン　ショウです
	watashi wa jane shaw dess

what is your name?	お名前は何ですか
	o-namae wa nan dess ka?
how are you?	お元気ですか
	o-genki dess ka?
fine thanks, and you?	元気です，あなたは
	genki dess, otaku wa?
I'm here on holiday	休暇でここにいます
	kyūka de koko ni imass
I'm here on business	仕事でここにいます
	shigoto de koko ni imass
this is my first trip to Japan	日本は初めてです
	nihon wa hajimete dess
this is my first trip to Tokyo	東京は初めてです
	tōkyō wa hajimete dess

• Gift-exchanging is very important in Japan and there are a few useful points to remember.

• If you are invited to someone's home, remember to take a gift, preferably something from your own country. Take care to wrap it as prettily as possible, even if it isn't expensive. Take more gifts than you think you could possibly need!

• When you receive a gift, you should show how delighted you are and even ask for a photo to be taken of you, your hosts and the gift.

have you ever been abroad?	外国にいった事がありますか
	gaikok ni itta koto ga arimass ka?
I enjoyed that very much	大変楽しかったです
	taihen tanoshikatta dess
that was a feast!	ごちそうさまでした!
	go-chisō-sama deshta!
thank you so much	ありがとうございます
	arigatō gozaimass

that was very kind of you, many thanks	お世話になりました。ありがとうございます
	o-sewa ni narimashta, arigatō gozaimashta
I'm going out	いってきます
	itte kimass
(reply to this)	いってらっしゃい
	itte rasshai
it was very nice to meet you	お会いできて楽しかったです
	o-ai dekite tanoshikatta dess
this is my address	私の住所です
	watashi no jūsho dess
this is my phone number	私の電話番号です
	watashi no denwa-bango dess

Money

Money – changing

• Japan is still largely a cash society, especially outside the big cities where it is more difficult to get cash.
• Banks are open 9am–3pm Monday–Friday and closed Saturdays, Sundays and on public holidays.
• Foreign currency can be changed only at banks with the sign 'Authorized Foreign Exchange Bank'. Citibank is the most orientated to dealing with foreigners.

where is the nearest bank?	一番近い銀行はどこですか
	ichiban chikai ginkō wa doko dess ka?
where is the nearest bureau de change?	一番近い両替所はどこですか
	ichiban chikai ryōgae-jo wa doko dess ka?
where is the cash machine?	銀行のATMはどこですか
	ginkō no ATM wa doko dess ka?
please show me	見せてください
	misete kudasai
I would like to change ... into yen	…を円に換えて下さい
	…o en ni kaetai dess
British pounds	イギリスポンド
	igiriss pondo
US/Australian/ dollars	アメリカ/オーストラリア/ドル
	amerika/ostoraria/doru
what is the rate for...?	…レートはいくらですか
	…rēto wa ikura dess ka?

please change this	これを替えて下さい
	kore o kaete kudasai
can I get cash with this credit card?	このクレジットカードで現金を引き出せますか
	kono krejitto kādo de genkin o hiki-dasemass ka?

Money – spending

- Credit cards are accepted in most hotels, shops and restaurants nowadays.
- Cash machines (ATM) are widespread but many don't accept cards of non-Japanese banks.
- If you plan to travel outside main cities, make sure you take cash.
- A 5% consumption tax is added to prices, except for tickets, newspapers and stamps. So for a 100-yen item, you pay 105 yen.

the bill please	お勘定お願いします
	o-kanjō onegai shimass
how much is it?	いくらですか
	ikura dess ka?
do I pay in advance?	前払いできますか
	maebarai dess ka?
where do I pay?	どこで払えばいいですか
	doko de haraeba ī dess ka?
can I pay with this credit card?	このクレジットカードで払えますか
	kono krejitto-kādo de haraemass ka?
can I pay with these traveller's cheques?	このトラベルチェックで払えますか
	kono toraberāzu chekk de haraemass ka?
please give me a receipt	レシートをお願いします
	reshīto o onegai shimass
please give me an itemized bill	明細をおねがいします
	meisai o onegai shimass

Is service included?	サービス料は含まれていますか
	saabisu-ryoo wa fukumarete imasu ka?
Is tax included?	税金は含まれていますか
	zeikin wa fukumarete imasu ka?
I will pay for this	私が払います
	watashi ga haraimass
this is on me!	私のおごりです!
	watashi no ogori dess!
I'm sorry	すみません
	sumimasen
I've nothing smaller	細かいお金を持っていません
	komakai okane o motte imasen
(no change)	小銭がありません
	kozeni ga arimasen

Getting around

Airport

• •

- Most signs will be in Japanese and English.
- Most people working at the airport will understand and speak some English.
- There are tourist information centres at the main airports.
- Visit **www.narita-airport.jp.en** for info.
- You can exchange your Japan Rail voucher at Narita International airport and use the Japan Rail Pass on the Narita Express into Tokyo.

to the airport please	空港までお願いします kūkō made onegai shimass
how do I get into town?	街までどうやって行けばいいですか machi made dōyatte ikeba ī dess ka?
where is the information desk?	案内所はどこですか annai-sho wa doko dess ka?
where is the JR ticket information office?	JRの旅行窓口はどこですか JR no ryokō mado-guchi wa doko dess ka?
where is the train to...?	...行きの電車はどこですか ...yuki no densha wa doko dess ka?
where is the bus to...?	...行きのバスはどこですか ...-yuki no bass wa doko dess ka?
where is the check-in desk for...?	...のチェックインカウンターはどこですか ...no chekk-in kauntā wa doko dess ka?

Customs and passports

- UK, US, Canadian and Australian visitors to Japan do not require a visa for short business trips and holidays.
- Visit **www.narita-airport-customs.go.jp** to find out about allowances.
- Japanese law requires you to carry proof of identity at all times, so make sure that you always carry your passport.
- Innoculations aren't required unless arriving from an infected area.
- Drug penalties in Japan are extremely high.

my passport	私のパスポート
	watashi no passpōto
my visa	私のビザ
	watashi no biza
I have ... nationality	…国籍です
	…kokseki dess
British/Australian/ US	イギリス/オーストラリア/アメリカ
	igiriss/ōstoraria/amerika
I came here on holiday	休暇でここにきました
	kyūka de koko ni kimashta
I came here on business	仕事でここにきました
	shigoto de koko ni kimashta
I have nothing to declare	申告する物はありません
	shinkok suru mono wa arimasen
the children are on this passport	子供たちもこのパスポートです
	kodomotachi mo kono passpōto
this is the baby's passport	これは子供のパスポートです
	kore wa kodomo no passpōto dess
it's a present	プレゼントです
	prezento dess
it's for my personal use	私が使う物です
	watashi ga tsukau mono dess

Asking the way – questions

• When asking directions in public, approach younger people if possible. Older people are likely to become flustered if addressed by a foreigner.
• Almost all street names are written in Japanese script only.
• Before you go anywhere, ask a Japanese person to write down the address, the nearest station or bus stop, the phone number and name of your host and draw a small map in Japanese. You can then ask for directions if you get lost.

excuse me	すみません sumimasen
please can you help me	助けて下さい taskete kudasai
I am looking for this address (point to written address)	この住所まで行きたいのですが kono jūsho made ikitai dess ga
where's the nearest...?	一番近い … はどこですか ichiban chikai … wa doko dess ka?
is it far?	遠いですか tōi dess ka?
how do I get there?	どう行けばいいですか dō ikeba ī dess ka?
how many kilometres is it?	何キロですか nan kiro dess ka?
please draw me a map	地図を書いて下さい chizu o kaite kudasai
how do I get to the...?	…にはどう行けばいいですか …niwa dō ikeba ī dess ka?
park	公園 kōen

temple	お寺
	o-tera
shrine	神社
	jinja
we're lost	道に迷いました
	michi ni mayoimashta
we're looking for...	...を探してます
	...o sagashte imass

Asking the way – answers

• If you are meeting someone, arrange to meet at a prominent building or in a hotel lobby.
• Note that **furonto** in Japanese means the front desk and not the front of the hotel.
• If you are completely lost, phone the Japan Help-Line 0120 461 997. This is a freephone number.
• Shopkeepers or policemen in the local police box (**koban**) may be able to help if you show them the written address.

east	東
	higashi
west	西
	nishi
north	北
	kita
south	南
	minami
exit	出口
	deguchi
entrance	入口
	iriguchi

central exit/ entrance	中央出口/入口	chūō deguchi/iriguchi
keep going straight ahead	真っ直ぐ行ってください	mas-sugu itte kudasai
the first	最初の	saisho no
the second	次を	tsugi o
on the right	右に	migi ni
on the left	左に	hidari ni
you have to turn round	引き帰してください	hiki kaeshte kudasai
keep going	そのまま進んでください	sono mama susunde kudasai
as far as...	...まで	...made
as far as the church	教会まで	kyōkai made
turn left	左に	hidari ni
turn right	右に	migi ni

Bus

• On some buses you enter at the front and pay as you enter.
• On others you enter by a middle door, taking a ticket from a machine either side of the door. This has a number on it. A display board at the front of the bus tells you your fare when you get off. A machine near the driver gives change.
• Display boards show the next bus (in **kanji**). Write down your destination so that you can recognize it. The name of the next stop is also displayed electronically inside the bus.

does this bus go to...?	このバスは … に行きますか
	kono bass wa … ni ikimass ka?
I want to go to...	…に行きたいです
	…ni ikitai dess
how long does it take by bus?	バスでどのくらいかかりますか
	bass de dono kurai kakarimass ka?
is the next bus stop...?	次のバス停は … ですか
	tsugi no bass tei wa … dess ka?
please tell me when we've at...	…についたら教えてください
	…ni tsuitara, oshiete kudasai
please, let me get off	すみません　降ろして下さい
	sumimasen, oroshte kudasai
sorry, I forgot to take a ticket	すみません、
	整理券を取りませんでした
(on entering bus)	sumimasen, seiriken o torimasen deshta
I got on at...	…から乗りました
	…kara norimashta

Subway

• Don't sit on the 'silver seats' marked in Japanese and English. These are reserved for the elderly and disabled.

• Many stations are multistorey and link with shopping malls, so there are many levels which can be confusing.

• Avoid the rush hour crush (7–9am and 5–8pm). There are women-only carriages on some lines during certain hours, to avoid any danger of groping hands.

• Don't put your feet on seats, and eating and drinking is forbidden on public transport (both on trains and in the station).

where is the subway station?	地下鉄の駅はどこですか chikatets no eki wa doko dess ka?
do you have a subway map?	地下鉄の地図はありますか chikatets no chizu wa arimass ka?
I want to go to...?	…へ行きたいです …e ikitai dess
can I go by subway?	地下鉄でいけますか chikatets de ikemass ka?
do I have to change?	乗り換えますか norikaemass ka?
where?	どこですか doko dess ka?
which line is it for ...?	…行きは何番線ですか …yuki wa nan–ban sen dess ka?
what's the next stop?	次の駅はなんですか tsugi no eki wa nan dess ka?
which station is it for Ueno?	上野に行くには、どの駅ですか ueno ni iku ni wa dono eki dess ka?
how do I buy a ticket? (from machine)	どうやって切符を買えばいいですか dō yatte kipp o kaeba ī dess ka?

I'm going to...   ...へ行きます

...e ikimass

Train

• •

• The Japan Rail Pass represents fabulous value for money. It is available to overseas visitors but a voucher for it must be purchased outside Japan (visit **www.japanrailpass.net** for more details).
• Passes are available for one, two or three weeks.
• The pass starts operating from the minute you exchange the voucher. So if you plan to spend four weeks in Japan but want to travel only the first and last weeks, buy two separate week passes.

where is the station?	駅はどこですか
	eki wa doko dess ka?
to the station please	駅までお願いします
	eki made onegai shimass
where is the ticket office?	切符売り場はどこですか
	kipp uriba wa doko dess ka?
how much does it cost to...?	...までいくらですか
	...made ikura dess ka?
I'm going to...	...へ行きます
	...e ikimass
a single	片道
	katamichi
2 singles	片道二枚
	katamichi nimai
a child's single	子供片道
	kodomo katamichi
a return	往復
	ōfku
2 returns	往復二枚
	ōfku nimai

a child's return	子供往復
	kodomo ōfku
a single to Nara please	奈良へ片道切符をください
	nara e katamichi kipp o kudasai
2 returns to Nara	奈良へ往復切符を二枚ください
	nara e ōfku kipp nimai kudasai
1st class	一等席
	ittō seki
2nd class	二等席
	nitō seki
smoking	喫煙
	kitsuen
non smoking	禁煙
	kin-en

● You can exchange the voucher at the JR office at Narita Airport and use the pass on the Narita Express to the centre of Tokyo.
● For local trains you would buy tickets at the automatic machines. You need to know the **kanji** for your destination and have some change. 200 and 100 yen are particularly useful. There is a route map on the ticket machine and the price to each destination shown under the name. Insert your money and get a ticket to that value (rather than to that destination).

do you have a train timetable?	時刻表はありますか
	jikoku-hyō wa arimass ka?
which is the platform for...?	...行きは何番線ですか
	...-yuki wa nan-ban-sen dess ka?
is this the train for...?	この電車は ... 行きですか
	kono densha wa ... yuki dess ka?
does this train stop at...?	この電車は ... で止まりますか
	kono densha wa ... de tomarimass ka?
please tell me when we arrive at...?	...についたら教えて下さい
	...ni tsuitara, oshiete kudasai

where is the exit for...?	...への出口はどこですか
	...e no deguchi wa doko dess ka?
is this seat free?	この席は空いてますか
	kono seki wa aete-imass ka?

Taxi

• Japanese taxis are safe, clean and metered. There is no need to tip.
• Most taxi drivers won't speak English, so have your destination written down in **kanji**.
• The driver operates the doors which open and close automatically including the boot. You leave by the kerbside, never into the traffic.

where can I get a taxi?	タクシー乗場はどこですか
	takshī noriba wa doko dess ka?
please go to...?	...へ行って下さい
	...e itte kudasai
to the airport please	空港までお願いします
	kūkō made onegai shimass
here is the address	これが住所です
	kore ga jūsho dess
to the station please	駅までお願いします
	eki made onegai shimass
please go here (point on map)	ここへ行って下さい
	koko e itte kudasai
how much will it cost to...?	...まではいくらですか
	...made wa ikura dess ka?
how long will it take?	どのくらいかかりますか
	dono kurai kakarimass ka?
please can I have a receipt	レシートお願いします
	reshīto o onegai shimass
please order me a taxi	タクシーを呼んでください
	takshī o yonde kudasai

Boat

●●●

● Japan Railways (JR) run some ferry services and on certain routes the JR Rail Pass can be used.
● There is a good ferry network in Japan linking the various islands. Ferries can be used as an alternative to trains if you wish to travel between the islands and have time to spare. The cheapest form of accommodation on boats travelling overnight is to sleep on the communal **tatami** mat floor.
● Boat trips are common from coastal towns for dolphin-watching, etc.

do you have a timetable?	時刻表はありますか jikoku-hyō wa arimass ka?
1 ticket/2 tickets	チケット一枚/チケット二枚 chiketto ichimai/chiketto nimai
single	片道 katamichi
round trip	往復 ōfku
are there any boat trips?	遊覧船はありますか kankō-sen wa arimass ka?
how long is the trip?	遊覧にはどのくらい時間がかかりますか kankō ni wa dono kurai jikan ga kakarimass ka?
when is the next boat?	次の船は何時ですか tsugi no fune wa nan-ji dess ka?
when does the boat leave?	船は何時にでますか fune wa nan-ji ni demass ka?
when does the ferry leave?	フェリーは何時に出ますか ferī wa nan-ji ni demass ka?

Car

Driving

- Visitors need an international driver's licence and their own.
- You drive on the left in Japan.
- The best roads are expressways (signposted in green). These are toll roads and expensive. Speed limits vary. Always check the signage.
- Some service stations on expressways just have toilets and vending machines for drinks and snacks.

can I park here?	ここに駐車できますか
	koko ni chūsha dekimass ka?
where can I park?	どこに駐車できますか
	doko ni chūsha dekimass ka?
is there a car park?	駐車場はありますか
	chusha jō wa arimass ka?
how long can I park here?	ここに何時間駐車できますか
	koko ni nan-jikan chūsha dekimass ka?
we're going to...?	...に行きます
	...ni ikimass
we're going to Nara	奈良に行きます
	nara ni ikimass
what's the best route?	どのルートが一番いいですか
	dono rūto ga ichiban ī dess ka?
how do I get onto the motorway?	どこから高速に乗ればいいですか
	doko kara kōsoku ni noreba ī dess ka?
which exit do I take for...?	...へはどの出口で下りればいいですか
	...e wa dono deguchi de orireba ī dess ka?

Petrol

• Petrol is cheaper than in the UK and the major companies have petrol stations.
• There is no self-service at petrol stations. Several people will come up to your car. One will ask how much petrol you want, another will clean the windscreen and someone else will clean your ashtray. Once you are ready to leave, they will usually stop the traffic for you to get on to the main road!
• The word 'gasoline' is widely understood, 'petrol' is unknown.

where is the nearest filling station?	一番近いガソリンスタンドはどこですか
	ichiban chikai gasorīn stando wa doko dess ka?
fill it up please	満タンでお願いします
	mantan de onegai shimass
3000 yen's worth of petrol	ガソリンを三千円分
	gasorin o san-zen en bun
that's my car (over there)	あれが私の車です
	are ga watashi no kuruma dess
this is my car (right here)	これが私の車です
	kore ga watashi no kuruma dess
where is the air line?	エアーはどこですか
	eya wa doko dess ka?
where is the water?	水はどこですか
	mizu wa doko dess ka?
please check...?	...をチェックして下さい
	...o chekk shte kudasai
the tyre pressure	タイヤの空気圧
	taiya no kuki–ats
the oil/the water	オイル/水
	oiru/mizu

Problems/breakdown

••

• The Japan Automobile Federation (JAF) is equivalent to the AA. Visit their website on **www.jaf.or.jp/e/index_e.htm**
• The JAF publishes a 'Rules of the Road' guide in English to help foreign drivers in Japan. These are available at JAF offices throughout Japan. Visit the website for addresses.
• If you break down, try to phone from an emergency roadside phonebox. This allows the JAF recovery service to pinpoint your location. Have ready the model, colour and registration of the car.

my car has broken down	車が故障しました
	kuruma ga koshō shimashta
what do I do?	どうすればいいですか
	dō sureba ī dess ka?
I'm on my own	私は一人です
	watashi wa hitori dess
I have children in the car	子供が車にいます
	kodomo ga kuruma ni imass
where is the nearest garage?	一番近い修理工場はどこですか
	ichiban chikai shuri kōjō wa doko dess ka?
is it serious?	ひどい故障ですか
	hidoi kosho dess ka?
can you repair it?	直せますか
	naosemass ka?
the car won't start	車が動きません
	kuruma ga ugokimasen
I have a flat tyre	タイヤがパンクしました
	taiya ga panku shimashta
the engine is overheating	エンジンがオーバーヒートしました
	enjin ga ōbahīto shimashta
the battery is flat	バッテリがなくなりました
	batterī ga naku-narimashta

have you got the parts?	パーツはありますか
	pāts wa arimass ka?
it's not working	動きません
	ugokimasen

Car hire

• Car rental firms are normally found near railway stations.
You can also book on-line with many of the big worldwide firms.
• Rental fees generally cover insurance and unlimited mileage.
• Half-day hires are available, but one-way rentals are expensive.
• Small cars are cheaper to rent and more practical for negotiating
city traffic and narrow country lanes.

where is the nearest car rental firm?	一番近いレンタカーの店はどこですか
	ichiban chikai rentakā no mise wa doko dess ka?
I'd like to rent a car	車を借りたいです
	kuruma o karitai dess
for one day	一日で
	ichi nichi de
for a week	一週間で
	isshūkan de
what are your rates...?	…料金はいくらですか
	…ryōkin wa ikura desu ka?
how much is the deposit?	保証金はいくらですか
	hoshōkin wa ikura desu ka?
do you take credit cards?	クレジットカードは使えますか
	kurejitto kādo wa tsukaemasu ka?
is there a charge per mile/ kilometre?	走行距離の支払いはありますか
	sōkō-kyori no siharai wa arimasu ka?

how much is it?	いくらですか
	ikura desu ka?
does the price include fully comprehensive insurance?	この金額は総合保険料を含んでいますか
	kono kingaku wa sōgōhoken-ryō o fukunde imasu ka?
I would like a small car	小型車が欲しいです
	kogata-sha ga hoshī dess
I would like a large car	大型車が欲しいです
	ogata-sha ga hoshī dess
I would like to rent this car	この車を借りたいです
	kono kuruma o karitai dess
where is the nearest petrol station?	ガソリンスタンドはどこにありますか
	gasorin sutando wa doko ni arimass ka
please explain the controls	操作を教えて下さい
	sōsa o oshiete kudasai
what do we do if we break down?	もし壊れたらどうすればいいですか
	moshi kowaretara dō sureba ī dess ka?
when must I return the car by?	いつまでに車を返せばいいですか
	itsu made ni kuruma o kaeseba ī dess ka?

Shopping

Shopping

....

- Shopping is a national pastime in Japan!
- Some shops are open 7 days a week from 10am to 8pm, but others close one day per week.
- Department stores close slightly earlier on Sundays. They offer free gift-wrapping services.
- Japanese value hand-made goods very highly – they also cost significantly more. Prices of simple items may shock you.
- VAT on shopping will be refunded at the airport if you complete the necessary forms.

do you sell...?	…はありますか
	…wa arimass ka?
stamps	切手
	kitte
where can I buy...?	…はどこで買えますか
	…wa doko de kaemass ka?
postcards	絵葉書
	e-hagaki
film	フィルム
	firumu
10 stamps	切手十枚
	kitte jumai
for postcards	絵葉書の
	e-hagaki no
to Britain	イギリスまで
	igiriss made

to United States	アメリカへ
	Amerika e
to Australia	オーストラリアへ
	Ōsutoraria e
when does the shop open?	店は何時に開きますか
	mise wa nan-ji ni akimass ka?
when does the shop close?	店は何時に閉まりますか
	mise wa nan-ji ni shimarimass ka?
I'm looking for a present	プレゼントを探しています
	prezento o sagashte imass
please show me that	それを見せて下さい
	sore o misete kudasai
this	これ
	kore
that (by you)	それ
	sore
that (over there)	あれ
	are

• Cameras, radios, etc. will often be cheaper in Japan and you usually find the latest designs, often months ahead of UK release dates. However, be warned that the instructions are often only in Japanese.

• You can buy wonderful gifts from local malls, supermarkets and 100-yen stores. (This will appal your Japanese friends!)
• It is generally difficult to find large sizes of clothes and shoes for men and women.

how much does this cost?	これはいくらですか
	kore wa ikura dess ka?
please write down the price	値段を書いて下さい
	nedan o kaite kudasai
it's too expensive	高すぎます
	takasugimass

I like this	これがすきです
	kore ga ski dess
I don't like it	好きではありません
	ski dewa arimasen
can I try it on?	試着できますか
	shichaku dekimass ka?
I'll buy this one	これを買います
	kore o kaimass
please wrap it for me (regular)	包んで下さい
	tsutsunde kudasai
please gift-wrap it for me	贈り物にして下さい
	okurimono ni shte kudasai
please show me a ... one	...を見せて下さい
	...no o misete kudasai
larger	もっと大きい
	motto ōkī
smaller	もっと小さい
	motto chīsai
newer	もっと新しい
	motto atarashī
more expensive	もっと高い
	motto takai
cheaper	もっと安い
	motto yasui

Shopping – food

- Vending machines are everywhere and very useful. You can get hot or cold tea, books, tights, etc. Ones selling alcohol shut down late at night until early morning.
- Most areas have a convenience store (**conbini**) which is open 24 hours and sells just about everything.
- You can buy pre-packed **o-bentō** (lunchboxes), which come complete with disposable chopsticks, in most supermarkets. There are also shops selling **hoka hoka bentō** (hot lunchboxes).

where can I buy...?	...はどこで買えますか
	...wa doko de kaemass ka?
fruit	果物
	kudamono
bread	パン
	pan
where is the supermarket?	スーパーはどこですか
	sūpā wa doko dess ka?
where is the baker's?	パン屋はどこですか
	pan-ya wa doko dess ka?
where is the market?	市場はどこですか
	ichiba wa doko dess ka?
a litre of...?	...一リットル
	...o ichi littōru
milk	牛乳
	gyūnyū
beer	ビール
	bīru
water	水
	mizu
a bottle of...	...一本
	o ... ippon

wine	ワイン
	wain
beer	ビール
	biru
water	水
	mizu
a can of...	...缶
	ohito ... kan
coke	コーラ
	kōra
beer	ビール
	bīru
water	水
	mizu
a packet of...	...1パック
	o ... wan–pak
biscuits	ビスケット
	bisketto
sugar	砂糖
	satō

- You must be over 20 to buy cigarettes and alcohol in Japan.
- Most food sold at supermarkets is pre-weighed and pre-wrapped. You just choose what you want and take it to the check-out.
- The fish market in Tokyo is well-worth visiting for the wonderful array of fish on display.
- The take-away counter at good supermarkets (and basements of department stores) can provide excellent, though expensive, meals.

a kilo of...	...一キロ
	o ... ichi kiro
cheese	チーズ
	chizu o

ham	ハム	
	hamu o	
200 grams of...	...二百グラム	
	o ... ni-hyaku guram	
butter	バター	
	batā o	
mince	ミンチ	
	minchi o	
potatoes	ジャガイモ	
	jaga imo	
apples	りんご	
	ringo	
8 slices of...	...を八枚	
	...o hachi mai	
ham	ハム	
	hamu	
salami	サラミ	
	sarami	
a loaf of bread	パン一個	
	pan ikko	
a baguette	フランスパン１本	
	furans pan ippon	
a tin of...	...の缶	
	...no kan	
tomatoes	トマト	
	tomato	
peas	グリーンピース	
	gurīn pīs	
a jar of...	...のビン	
	...no bin	
jam	ジャム	
	jamu	
honey	蜂蜜	
	hachi-mits	

Daylife

Sightseeing

• •

• The Japan National Tourist Organization website
(**www.jnto.go.jp**) is excellent for practical information and for
helping you find accommodation, transport, etc.
• Tourist Info Centers (TIC) have maps and leaflets in English.
• If you plan to go off the beaten track, book accommodation in
advance – you're unlikely to find people who speak English.
• Entrance to museums and galleries is usually about US$10.

excuse me, where is the tourist office?	すみません、観光案内所はどこですか sumimasen, kankō annai-sho wa doko dess ka?
where is the...?	…はどこですか …wa doko dess ka?
museum	博物館 hakubutsu-kan
castle	城 shiro
park	公園 kōen
temple	寺 tera
shrine	神社 jinja
we want to visit...?	私たちは … 行きたい watashi tachi wa … ikitai

have you any leaflets?	パンフレットはありますか
	panfretto wa arimass ka?
is it open to the public?	一般公開していますか
	ippan kōkai shteimass ka?
how much is it to get in?	入場料はいくらですか
	nyūjō-ryo wa ikura dess ka?
is there a bus tour?	観光バスツアーはありますか
	kankō-bass tsuā wa arimass ka?
when does it leave?	いつ出発しますか
	itsu shuppats shimass ka?
where does it leave from?	どこから出ますか
	doko kara demass ka?

● Beware of an overdose of temples and shrines! Particularly on guided tours.

● Major festivals are not the best times to travel around Japan. The transport system gets clogged up with people going home – particularly at Golden Week (end April/beginning of May, and **Obon** (mid-August).

● Public holidays falling on a Sunday are celebrated that day. The following Monday becomes a public holiday.

what time does the tour leave?	ツアーは何時に出発しますか
	tsuā wa nan-ji ni shuppats shimass ka?
are there reductions for...?	...の割引はありますか
	...no waribiki wa arimass ka?
students/children/ seniors	学生/子供/老人
	gaksei/kodomo/rō-jin
what time does it open?	何時に開きますか
	nan-ji ni akimass ka?
what time does it close?	何時に閉まりますか
	nan-ji ni shimarimass ka?
how much is the entry fee?	入場料はいくらですか
	nyūjō-ryo wa ikura dess ka?

where can I buy postcards?	どこで絵葉書を買えますか
	doko de e-hagaki o kaemass ka?
where can I buy souvenirs?	どこでお土産を買えますか
	doko de o-miyage o kaemass ka?

Sport and leisure

• The Japan National Tourist Organization has details on sport. Visit their website **www.jnto.go.jp**.
• Some golf clubs welcome overseas visitors. Contact the JNTO for details. Golf is used to cement business relationships.
• You can practise your golf swing at a driving range. These are often multistorey or on the tops of buildings.
• Skiing in Japan is expensive – contact the JNTO for details.

where can we do...?	どこで ... ができますか
	doko de ... ga dekimass ka?
tennis	テニス
	tenis
golf	ゴルフ
	gorufu
riding	乗馬
	jōba
fishing	釣り
	tsuri
where can we go hiking?	どこでハイキングができますか
	doko de haikingu ga dekimass ka?
do I need walking boots?	登山靴が必要でしょうか
	tozan-kutsu ga hitsuyō deshō ka?
where can we go swimming?	どこか泳げるところはありますか
	doko-ka oyogeru tokoro wa arimass ka?
where can we play golf?	どこでゴルフができますか
	doko de gorufu ga dekimass ka?

can we rent the equipment?	用具はレンタルできますか yōgu wa rentaru dekimass ka?

• **Sumo** is a hugely popular spectator and tv sport. It takes place in different cities across Japan. If you are staying in a city hosting a tournament it is worth visiting the **Sumo Beya** (literally 'stable') where you can see the wrestlers practise.
• You can generally swim in the sea from July to mid-August. From mid-August the coastal waters become infested with jellyfish. You need a swimming cap in public pools.

can I hire...?	...借りれますか ...kariremass ka?
rackets	ラケット raketto
golf clubs	ゴルフクラブ gorufu kurab
I am a beginner	初心者です shoshinsha dess
how much is it per hour?	一時間でいくらですか ichi-jikan de ikura dess ka?
how much is it per day?	一日でいくらですか ichi-nichi de ikura dess ka?
is there a soccer match?	サッカーの試合はありますか sakkā no shiai wa arimass ka?
where do I buy tickets?	チケットはどこで買えますか chiketto wa doko de kaemass ka?
can we take lessons?	レッスンを受けれますか ressun o ukeremass ka?
where is there a sports shop?	スポーツ店はどこですか supōtsu ten wa doko dess ka?

Nightlife

Nightlife

• Major tour operators run fixed-price night tours to the more expensive nightclubs and cabarets. Ask at the Tourist Information Centre.
• Cherry blossom time is when people go to the parks (usually at night) to admire the blossom and drink alcohol.
• Some bars are run by the big brewery firms, these include **Suntory**, **Asahi** and **Kirin**.
• Beware of cover charges, which can be very expensive.

what is there to do at night?	夜遊べるところはありますか
	yoru asoberu tokoro wa arimass ka?
which is a good bar?	いいバーはどこですか
	ī bar wa doko dess ka?
is it expensive?	そこは高いですか
	soko wa takai dess ka?
which is a good disco?	いいデイスコはどこですか
	ī disko wa doko dess ka?
where can we hear live music?	どこでライブ音楽が聞けますか
	doko de raibu ongaku ga kikemass ka?
are there any concerts?	コンサートはありますか
	konsāto wa arimass ka?
we want to go to a karaoke bar	カラオケに行きたいです
	karaoke ni ikitai dess
are there any local festivals?	地元の祭りはありますか
	jimoto no matsuri wa arimass ka?

- **Karaoke** bars are very popular. Don't refuse a turn at the microphone if you are asked!
- Visit **www.jnto.go.jp** for information on local festivals. **Obon** is a national festival and is celebrated in mid-August. There are often impressive firework displays.
- Prices for the theatre and concerts tend to be high. You should dress quite conservatively.

we'd like to go to the...?	...へ行きたいです ...ē ikitai dess
theatre	劇場 gekijō
opera	オペラ opera
ballet	バレー balay
a concert	コンサート konsāto
what's on?	今何か催しはありますか ima nanika moyōshi wa arimass ka?
do I need to book?	予約が要りますか yoyaku ga irimass ka?
how much are the tickets?	チケットはいくらですか chiketto wa ikura dess ka?
2 tickets...	...チケット二枚 ...chiketto nimai
for tonight	今夜の konya no
for tomorrow night	明日の夜の ashta no yoru no
for 5th August	8月5日の hachi-gats itsuka no
when does the performance end?	この公演は何時終りますか kono kōen wa itsu owarimass ka?

Accommodation

Hotel

. . . .

- The Japan National Tourist Organization and Tourist Information Centers can help with finding accommodation. Visit **www.jnto.go.jp**.
- Japan offers a wide choice of places to stay – from western-style hotels to traditional inns (**ryokan**).
- Capsule hotels comprise tiny, self-contained cubicles stacked on top of each other, with shared bath facilities. There are vending machines for food, drink and toiletries. They are good value.

where is the nearest hotel?	一番近いホテルはどこですか ichiban chikai hoteru wa doko dess ka?
have you a room for tonight?	今夜部屋はありますか konya heya wa arimass ka?
single	シングル shinguru
double	ダブル daburu
family room	ファミリールーム famirī rūm
with bath	バス付 bāss tsuki
with shower	シャワー付 shawā tsuki
I/we will be staying...	...します ...shimass
one night	一泊 ippak

2 nights/3 nights	二泊/三泊
	nihak/sanpak
how much is it per night?	一泊いくらですか
	ippak ikura dess ka?
is breakfast included?	朝食込みですか
	chōshoku komi dess ka?

- 'Love hotels' should not be thought of as sleazy. They allow Japanese couples (even married ones) some privacy. Rooms are hired for 2-hour periods in the day or for overnight stays. Rooms can be wonderfully decorated on fanciful themes!
- A **ryokan** is a traditional Japanese inn. The price usually includes dinner and breakfast.
- A **minshuku** is a cheaper version of a **ryokan**, usually bigger and only in main tourist areas.

I booked a room	部屋を予約しています
	heya o yoyak shteimass
my name is	…です
	…dess
my key please	カギを下さい
	kagi o kudasai
come in please!	入ってくださいどうぞ!
	haitte kudasai dōzo!
please come back later	後で来て下さい
	ato de kite kudasai
please call me…	…呼んで下さい
	…yonde kudasai
at 7 o'clock	７時に
	shichi-ji ni
is there a laundry service?	クリーニングサービスはありますか
	kurīningu sābis wa arimass ka?
I'm leaving tomorrow	明日出発します
	asu shuppats shimass

the bill please	お勘定をお願いします
	o-kanjō o onegai shimass
when is check-out time?	チェックアウトはいつですか
	chekk-aut wa itsu dess ka?

Self-catering

- Voltage throughout Japan is 100 volts.
- Most laptops, camera chargers etc. are 100-240 volts nowadays.
- Plugs are two-pronged.
- Rubbish must be separated into biodegradable, plastic, glass, tin, etc. Large items (e.g. furniture) can be put out once a month for collection.
- Visit **www.jnto.go.jp** for more information.

which is the key for this door?	どれがこのドアのカギですか
	dore ga kono doā no kagi dess ka?
please show us how this works	これはどうすればよいのか教えて下さい
	kore ga dō sureba yoi no ka oshiete kudasai
who do I contact if there are any problems?	問題がある時どこへ連絡すればいいですか
	mondai ga aru toki doko e renrak sureba ī dess ka?
we need extra...	...を余分にください
	...o yobun ni kudasai
cutlery	ナイフとフォーク
	naifu to fōku
sheets	シーツ
	sheets
the gas has run out	ガスが切れました
	gass ga kiremashta

what do I do?	どうすればいいですか
	dō sureba ī dess ka?
where is the	コインランドリーはどこですか
launderette?	koin randorī wa doko dess ka?
where do I put	ゴミはどこに置けばいいですか
the rubbish?	gomi wa doko ni okeba ī dess ka?

Camping and caravanning

● Official campsites often close during winter. They may be very full during July and August – visit **www.outdoorjapan.com** for information.

● The wet season in Japan is from early June to mid-July. The weather is hot and very muggy, causing clothes and books to get mouldy. It is always advisable to carry a small towel with you at all times and some water.

we're looking for	キャンプ場を探してます
a campsite	kyanpu-jo o sagashtemass
have you a list	キャンプ場のリストはありますか
of campsites?	kyanpu-jo no risto wa arimass ka?
where is the	キャンプ場はどこですか
campsite?	kyanpu-jo wa doko dess ka?
have you any	空きはありますか
vacancies?	aki wa arimass ka?
how much is it	一泊いくらですか
per night?	ippak ikura dess ka?
does the price	…の料金は含まれていますか
include...?	...no ryōkin wa fukumarete imasu ka?
showers	シャワー
	shawā
hot water	お湯
	oyu

electricity	電気 denki
we'd like to stay for ... nights	...泊したいです ...pak shtai dess
can we have a more sheltered site?	もっと風の当たらない場所はありますか motto kaze no ataranai basho wa arimass ka?
this site is very muddy	ここはとてもぬかるんでいます koko wa totemo nukarunde imass
is there another site?	他の所はありますか hoka no tokoro wa arimass ka?
is there a shop on the site?	お店はありますか o-mise wa arimass ka?
can we camp here?	ここでキャンプできますか koko de kyanpu dekimass ka?

Different travellers

Children

• Children between six and eleven pay half price on rail fares. There is also a child Japan Rail Pass.
• **www.tokyowithkids.com** has useful info.
• Children under six travel free on trains. However, if the train is crowded, they should sit on your lap.
• Some Japanese school children wear a distinctive 'sailor-type' uniform with hats.
• Older Japanese children have all the latest gadgets.

a child's ticket	子供のチケット kodomo no chiketto
he/she is ... years old	彼は/彼女は ... 歳です kare/kanojo wa ... sai dess
is there a reduction for children?	子供割引はありますか kodomo waribiki wa arimass ka?
do you have a children's menu?	子供用メニューありますか kodomo-yō menyū arimass ka?
what is there for children to do?	何か子供が楽しめるものはないでしょうか nani ka kodoma ga tanoshimeru mono wa nai deshō ka?
do you have...?	...ありますか ...arimass ka?
a high chair/ a cot	ベビーチェヤー/ベビーベッド baby cheyā/baby bed

I have two children	子供が二人います
	kodomo ga futari imass
do you have children?	子供がいますか
	kodomo ga imass ka?
is it safe for children?	子供に安全ですか
	kodomo ni anzen dess ka?

Special needs

● Public transport in Japan caters for disabled travellers with numerous escalators and elevators. There are clear markings on platforms to assist the visually impaired.
● Stations have a Braille board with station names and fares.
● You may need a member of staff to help you get a wheelchair on a train.
● Check out the website **www.tokyoessentials.com** for information on accessibility to hotels, shopping and museums.

what facilities do you have for disabled people?	障害者用の設備はありますか
	shōgaisha-yō no setsubi wa arimasu ka?
is it possible to visit ... with a wheelchair?	…に車椅子で行けますか
	…ni kuruma-iss de ikemass ka?
do you have toilets for the disabled?	障害者用のトイレがありますか
	shōgaisha-yō no toire ga arimass ka?
I need a bedroom on the ground floor	寝室が一階に欲しいです
	shinshitsu ga ikkai ni hoshī dess
is there a lift?	エレベーターはありますか
	erebētā ga arimass ka?
where is the lift?	エレベーターはどこですか
	erebētā wa doko dess ka?

I can't walk far	遠くまで歩けません
	tōku made arukemasen
are there many steps?	階段がたくさんありますか
	kaidan ga taksan arimass ka?
is there an entrance for wheelchairs?	車椅子の入口はありますか
	kuruma-iss no iriguchi wa arimass ka?
can I travel on this train with a wheelchair?	この電車に車椅子で乗れますか
	kono densha ni kuruma-iss de noremass ka?
do you have an induction loop?	誘導ループシステムはありますか
	yūdō rūpu shisutemu wa arimasu ka?
is there a reduction for disabled people?	障害者割引はありますか
	shōgaisha waribiki wa arimasu ka?
is there somewhere I can sit down?	どこか座れる所がありますか
	doko ka suwareru tokoro ga arimasu ka?

Exchange visitors

• These phrases are intended for families hosting Japanese-speaking visitors.
• If you receive a gift from a Japanese visitor, you should make a great fuss of it, expressing your delight at both its beautiful wrapping and contents.
• The Japanese are usually very quiet and self-effacing in public and dislike loudness and bad behaviour in others. It is probably worth keeping this in mind when you take any Japanese visitors out.

what would you like for breakfast?	朝食は何がいいですか
	chōshok wa nani ga ī dess ka?
what would you like to eat?	何を食べたいですか
	nani o tabetai dess ka?

what would you like to drink?	何を飲みたいですか
	nani o nomitai dess ka?
did you sleep well?	よく眠れましたか
	yoku nemuremashta ka?
would you like a shower?	シャワーを使いますか
	shawā o tsukaimass ka?
what would you like to do today?	今日は何をしたいですか
	kyō wa nani o shtai dess ka?
would you like to go shopping?	買い物に行きたいですか
	kaimono ni ikitai dess ka?
did you enjoy yourself?	楽しみましたか
	tanoshimimashta ka?
take care	気をつけて
	ki o tskete

- These phrases are intended for those people staying with Japanese-speaking families.
- Japan runs a Home Stays scheme where you can stay in family homes. Visit the Japan National Tourist Organization at **www.jnto.go.jp** for more details.
- Always remove shoes when entering someone's home or before stepping on **tatami** matting.
- Don't use special toilet slippers in other parts of the house.

I like...	私は … が好きです
	watashi wa … ga ski dess
I don't like...	私は … が好きではありません
	watashi wa … ga ski dewa arimasen
that was delicious	おいしかったです
	oishkatta dess
thank you very much	ありがとうございました
	arigatō gozaimashta
can I borrow...?	…を借りれますか
	…o kariremass ka?

an iron	アイロン
	airon
a hairdryer	ヘアドライヤー
	heā doraiyā
what time do I have to get up?	何時に起きなければなりませんか
	nan-ji ni okinakereba narimasen ka?
can you take me by car?	車で連れて行って頂けますか
	kuruma de tsurete itte itadakemass ka?
how long are you staying?	どのくらいいますか
	dono kurai imass ka?
I'm leaving in a week	一週間で出発します
	isshūkan de shuppats shimass
thanks for everything	お世話になりました
	osewa ni narimashta
I've had a great time	とても楽しかったです
	totemo tanoshikatta dess

Bathing

Bathing

- In a hotel you use a private bathroom as you would at home.
- If you are in someone's home, you must wash carefully before entering the bath. Soap should not get into the bathwater, which is often kept in the bath for hours, with a mat on top to keep the heat in. Don't pull out the plug!
- A visit to an **onsen** (natural spring) or a **sento** (public bath) is a must. Here you shower at the shower stools before you go in, washing yourself very thoroughly before entering the water.

may I take a bath?	お風呂に入ってもいいですか
	o-furo ni haittemo ī dess ka?
where is the bathroom?	お風呂はどこですか
	o-furo wa doko dess ka?
where is the toilet?	トイレはどこですか
	toire wa doko dess ka?
until when can I use the bath?	何時までお風呂に入れますか
	nan-ji made o-furo ni hairemass ka?
a large towel please	大きいタオルをください
	okī taoru o kudasai
the water is very hot!	お湯はとても熱いです！
	oyu wa totemo atsui dess!
this is very relaxing!	とても気持ちがいいです！
	totemo kimochi ga ī dess!
I like Japanese baths	日本のお風呂が好きです
	nihon no o-furo ga ski dess

Difficulties

Complaints

••

• Japan is a very honest society. There is very little crime.
• Most Japanese people will try to help you as much as they can.
Perhaps they are too helpful, in that they will try to give you
directions even if they are not sure themselves where the place is.
• Japanese people dislike loud behaviour. Shouting or raising your
voice would not be advisable in any situation, however frustrating
it may be.

the light	電気	
	denki	
the air conditioning	冷房	
	reibō	
...doesn't work	...が動きません	
	...ga tsukimasen	
there is no...	...がありません	
	...ga arimasen	
hot water	お湯	
	oyu	
toilet paper	トイレットペーパー	
	toiretto pēpā	
the room is dirty	部屋が汚いです	
	heya ga kitanai dess	
the bath is dirty	お風呂が汚いです	
	ofuro ga kitanai dess	
it is too noisy	うるさいです	
	urusai dess	

the room is too small	部屋が狭いです
	heya ga semai dess
this isn't what I ordered	注文と違います
	chūmon to chigaimass
I want to complain	苦情を申し立てます
	kujō o mōshitatemass
there is a mistake	間違いがあります
	machigai ga arimass
this is broken	これは壊れてます
	kore wa kowarete-imass
can you repair it?	これを直せますか
	kore o naosemass ka?

Problems

● Though English is Japan's second language, few Japanese have encountered a native English speaker in person.
● Information and help is available from the local Tourist Information Centers. These are usually located in or near major railway stations or town centres. Look out for the red question mark with the word 'information' underneath.
● The Japan Help Line number is 0120 461 997. This is a freephone number.

can you help me?	助けてくれますか
	taskete kuremass ka?
I don't speak Japanese	日本語を話せません
	nihongo o hanasemasen
do you speak English?	英語を話せますか
	eigo o hanashimass ka?
does anyone speak English?	誰か英語がわかりますか
	dareka eigo ga wakarimass ka?

please speak slowly	ゆっくり話してください
	yukkuri hanashte kudasai
I'm lost	道に迷ってしまいました
	michi ni mayotte shimaimashta
I'm late	遅れます
	okuremass
I need to get to...	...行かなければなりません
	...ikanakereba narimasen
plane	飛行機
	hikōki
flight connection	乗り継ぎ
	nori-tsugi
I've missed my...	...乗り遅れました
	...nori-okuremashta
my luggage has not arrived	私の荷物が着いてません
	nimots ga tsuitemasen

● If you are lost or need help, try asking a younger person for help. You might find an older person gets flustered.
● If you find that your spoken English is not understood, try writing it down clearly. Many Japanese have a good knowledge of written English.
● Ask the policeman in the local police box (**koban**) for help.
● As in any country, do not put yourself in danger. Do not leave valuables lying around and do be sensible.

money	お金
	okane
passport	パスポート
	passpōto
I've lost my...	...無くしました
	...naku shimashta
camera	私のカメラ
	kamera

keys	私のカギ
	kagi
I've left my bag in...	...に荷物を忘れました
	...ni nimots o wasuremashta
I have forgotten my...	...を忘れました
	...o wasuremashta
my ... is missing (thing)	私の … がなくなりました
	watashi no … ga naku-narimashta
I have no money	お金がありません
	okane ga arimasen
leave me alone!	私に構わないで!
	watashi ni kamawanaide!
go away!	あっちへ行って!
	acchi e itte!

Emergencies

• The word for help is **taskete!**
• There are often police boxes (**koban**) by main street crossings. They look after people in the street and help with directing them. They also receive lost property.
• If you have lost something, the chances are that you will get it back. Either go to the **koban** or ask at your hotel desk. If you have left something in a taxi, the driver will either take it back to your hotel or to the **koban**.

help!	助けて!
	taskete!
can you help me?	助けてくれますか
	taskete kuremass ka?
there's been an accident	事故がありました
	jiko ga arimashta

someone is injured	誰かがケガをしました
	dareka ga kega o shimashta
call...	...を呼んでください
	...o yonde kudasai
the police	警察
	keisats
an ambulance	救急車
	kyū-kyū-sha
the fire brigade	消防隊
	shōbō tai
he was driving too fast	彼はスピードを出しすぎました
	kare wa spīdo o dashisugimashta
I need a report for my insurance	保険のために報告書が要ります
	hoken no tame ni hōkokshō ga irimass
I've been robbed	盗難に遭いました
	tōnan ni aimashta

• The emergency numbers are 110 for the police and 119 for an ambulance or the fire brigade.
• There are lots of small earthquakes and typhoons in Japan. You might only notice them by the trees bending a lot or from flights being postponed.
• Some public phones have a red emergency button.
• Tourist Information Centers provide details of English-speaking hospitals, dentists and pharmacies.

please call the police	警察を呼んでください
	keisats o yonde kudasai
where is the nearest police station?	一番近い交番はどこですか
	ichiban chikai koban wa doko dess ka?
I'm being followed	つけられています
	tsukerarete-imass

I would like to call my embassy	大使館に電話をしたいです
	taishikan ni denwa o shtai dess
where is the ... consulate?	...領事館はどこですか
	...ryojikan wa doko dess ka?
British	イギリス
	igiriss
Australian	オーストラリア
	ōstoraria
Canadian	カナダ
	kanada
New Zealand	ニュージーランド
	nyū jīrando
US	アメリカ
	amerika
I have no money	お金がありません
	okane ga arimasen

Health

Health

••

• Healthcare for visitors to Japan is expensive – make sure your travel insurance has adequate medical coverage for your stay.
• You can go to the out-patients department of a hospital for treatment. You will have to pay, probably in cash.
• You cannot usually get foreign medicine in Japan.
• Pharmacists are very good. If you act out your complaint, draw it, or point to the area in question, a product will be found or you will be sent to hospital.

have you something for...?	…のために何かありますか
	…no tame ni nanika arimass ka?
a headache	頭痛
	zutsū
car sickness	車酔い
	kuruma yoi
a cough	咳
	seki
flu	インフルエンザ
	infurenza
diarrhoea	下痢
	geri
is it safe to give children?	これは子供に安全ですか
	kore wa kodomo ni anzen dess ka?
how much should I give him?	どれだけ飲ませればいいですか
	doredake nomasereba ī desu ka?

I don't feel well	気分が良くないです
	kibun ga yoku arimasen
I need a doctor	医者にかかりたいです
	isha ni kakaritai dess
my son/daughter is ill	息子/娘 が病気です
	musuko/musume ga byōki dess
he/she has a temperature	彼/彼女 は熱があります
	kare/kanojo wa nets ga arimass
I'm taking this medicine	この薬を飲んでいます
	kono kusuri o nonde-imass
I have high blood pressure	私は高血圧です
	watashi wa kō-ketsu-atsu dess
I'm pregnant	妊娠してます
	ninshin shteimass
I'm on the pill	ピルを飲んでいます
	piru o nonde-imass

● Tap water is drinkable throughout Japan.
● Condoms are available in supermarkets, chemists and most convenience stores.
● If you are put on antibiotics, make sure you get a full 10-day course and not the 5-day which seems favoured in Japan.
● Constipation is **bempi**. Ask for **bempi no kusuri**.

I'm allergic to penicillin	ペニシリンのアレルギーがあります
	penishirin ni arerugī ga arimass
my blood group is (O, A etc.)...	血液型は ... です
	ketsueki gata wa ... dess
I'm breastfeeding	授乳中です
	junyū-chū dess
can I take it?	これを飲んでもいいですか
	kore o nondemo ī dess ka?

will he/she have to go to hospital?	彼/彼女は病院に行かなければなりませんか
	kare/kanojo wa byōin ni ikanakereba narimasen ka?
when are visiting hours?	診療時間はいつですか
	shinryō-jikan wa itsu desu ka?
will I have to pay?	支払わなければいけませんか
	shiharawanakereba ikemasen ka?
how much will it cost?	いくらかかりますか
	ikura kakarimasu ka?
can you give me a receipt for the insurance?	保険のための領収書をもらえますか
	hoken no tame no ryōshūsho o moraemasu ka?
I need to go to A & E	救急病院に行きたいです
	kyū-kyū byōin ni ikitai dess
where is the hospital?	病院はどこですか
	byōin wa doko dess ka?
I need to see a dentist	歯医者に行きたいです
	haisha ni ikitai dess
I have toothache	歯が痛いです
	ha ga itai dess
the filling has come out	詰物が取れました
	tsumemono ga toremashta
it hurts	痛いです
	itai dess

Business

Business

• To cement ties, present-exchanging is important. These presents are company to company and may well be displayed in the offices. They may also be person to person.
• Have business cards (**meishi**) printed with your details in English on one side and Japanese on the other.
• Treat **meishi** with respect, read them carefully on receipt and say the name out loud. Then put the card in your wallet to show that you are putting it somewhere safe and for future reference.

I'm...	...です
	...dess
here's my card	私の名刺です
	watashi no meishi dess
I'm from Jones Ltd	私はJones 社の者です
	watashi wa Jones-sha no mono dess
I'd like to arrange a meeting with Mr/Ms...	...さんとお会いしたいので、予約をお願いします
	...-san to o-ai shtai no de, yoyaku o onegai shimass
on 4 May at 11 o'clock	5月4日の11時に
	go-gats yokka no jū ichi-ji ni
can we meet at a restaurant?	レストランでお会いできますか
	resutoran de aemass ka?
I will confirm by e-mail	メールで確認します
	e-meru de kakunin shimass

what's your e-mail address?	メールアドレスはなんですか
	mēru adoress wa nan dess ka?
is there a website?	ホームページはありますか
	hōmpēji wa arimass ka?
where can I plug in my laptop?	パソコンに繋ぐコンセントはどこですか
	pasukon ni tsunagu konsento wa doko dess ka?
what is your website address?	ホームページのアドレスを教えてください
	hōmupēji no adoress o oshiete kudasai

• Never say 'no'. Use other expressions such as **tsugō ga warui** ('that might be troublesome').
• The Japanese don't speak in long monologues. They leave little spaces in conversation to ensure you are following. Nod encouragement in these spaces with **hai** or **dess ne**.
• Dress smartly and conservatively – suits for men, skirts for women. Women should always wear tights (even in the most humid weather), and never wear open sandal shoes for business.

I'm staying at Hotel...	hotel ... に滞在してます
	hotel ... ni taizai shteimass
how do I get to your office?	そちらの会社への道順を教えてください
	sochira no kaisha e no michijun o oshiete kudasai
here is some information about my company	これは当社の会社概要です
	kore wa tōsha no kaisha gaiyō dess
I'm delighted to meet you	初めまして
	hajimemashte
my Japanese isn't very good	私は日本語が上手くありません
	watashi no nihongo wa umaku arimasen

I need an interpreter	通訳の方をお願いします
	tsūyak no kata o onegai shimass
I would like some information about the company	会社案内を頂けますか
	kaisha annai o itadakemass ka

Phoning

• •

- Public phones accept 10-yen and 100-yen coins or phonecards. It is best to use 10-yen coins for short calls as no refund is given if you only partially use the 100-yen coin.
- Phonecards can be bought at vending machines, kiosks and shops. There are cards for domestic use (which you just insert), and international cards where you follow instructions.
- Calls are cheaper at night and Saturdays, Sundays and national holidays.
- Numbers beginning 0120 and 0088 are freephone.

where can I buy a phonecard?	どこでテレホンカードを買えますか
	doko de terehon-kādo o kaemass ka?
a phonecard please	テレホンカードを下さい
	terehon kādo o kudasai
I want to make a phone call	電話をかけたいです
	denwa o kaketai dess
can I speak to...?	...はいらっしゃいますか
	...wa irasshaimass ka?
this is...	私は ... です
	kochira wa ... dess
Mr Tanaka please	田中さんをお願いします
	Tanaka san o onegai shimass
I'll call back later	あとでかけ直します
	ato de kake-naoshimass

do you have a mobile phone?	携帯電話はお持ちですか keitei denwa wa o-mochi dess ka?
what's your phone number?	電話番号を教えてください denwa-bangō o oshiete kudasai
I'll text you	携帯にメールします keitai ni mēru shimass
can you text me?	携帯にメールをしてくれませんか keitai ni mēru o shte kuremasen ka?

• You can make international phone calls from some public phones (look out for the international and domestic signs).
• Foreign mobiles won't work in Japan. You can hire mobile phones for your stay from Narita and Kansai airports.
• Direct calls can be made using a telephone company and dialling their access code. You can also use a credit card but you have to insert a 100-yen coin to dial the access company. The coin is then refunded.

this is my phone number	これが私の電話番号です kore ga watashi no denwa-bangō dess
hello! (used only on the telephone)	もしもし! moshi-moshi!
this is...	...です ...dess
may I speak to Mr/Mrs/Ms...	...さんを　お願いします ...-san o onegai shimass
I'll call back later	後でかけ直します ato de kake-naoshimass
please speak more slowly	もう少しゆっくり話してください mō sukoshi yukkuri hanashte kudasai
please repeat that	もう一度言ってください mō ichi-do itte kudasai
who is calling?	どなたですか donata dess ka?

please hold a moment	少々お待ちください
	shō-shō o-machi kudasai
please try again later	あとでおかけ直しください
	ato de o-kake-naoshi kudasai

Post office

• The Japanese mail system is efficient but fairly expensive.
• Post offices are open 9am–5pm, Monday–Friday. Some main post offices are open seven days a week.
• You can change money at large post offices.
• Letters can be addressed in **romaji** (western letters), but write clearly in block capitals.
• Mailboxes are red. If they have two slots, one is for regular mail, the other for express and international. You can find out postal rates at **www.jnto.go.jp** under Essential Info.

where is the nearest post office?	一番近い郵便局はどこですか
	ichiban chikai yūbin-kyok wa doko dess ka?
by airmail please	航空便でお願いします
	kōkūbin de onegai shimass
by registered mail please	書留でお願いします
	kakitome de onegai shimass
aerogrammes please	航空書簡を下さい
	kōkū shokan o kudasai
stamps please	切手を下さい
	kitte o kudasai
postcards please	絵葉書を下さい
	postokādo o kudasai
I want to send this parcel	この小包みを送りたいです
	kono ko-zutsumi o okuritai dess
to Europe/	ヨーロッパへ/オーストラリアへ/

Post office

to Australia/ to America	アメリカへ yōroppa e/ōstoraria e/amerika e
how much will it cost?	いくらですか ikura dess ka?
how long will it take?	どのくらいかかりますか dono kurai kakarimass ka?

E-mail/fax

• •

- Japanese website addresses end **.jp**.
- 'At' is used for the symbol @.
- The pronunciation for 'at' is **atto**.
- www. is said as in English.
- The international dialling code for Japan is oo81.
- English web addresses are understood.

I want to send an e-mail	eメイルを送りたいです e-mēru o okuritai dess
what's your e-mail address?	メールアドレスを教えてください mēru adoress o oshiete kudasai
my e-mail address is...	わたしのeメイルアドレスは ... です watashi no mēru adoress wa ... dess
how do you spell it?	綴りを教えてください tsuzuri o oshiete kudasai
all one word	一言 hito koto
all lower case (small letters)	全部小文字 Zenbu komoji
did you get my e-mail?	私のメールは届きましたか watashi no e-mail wa todokimashta ka?
I want to send a fax	faxを送りたいです fax o okuritai dess

do you have a fax?	faxはありますか
	fax wa arimass ka?
what is your fax number?	fax番号を教えてください
	fax bangō o oshiete kudasai

Internet/cybercafé

• •

• Computer and Internet terminology tends to be in English.

• Access to the internet is widely available in Japan. Almost all hotels, even in the countryside, now have at least one computer available for use by guests. Hotels in larger cities might also have network jacks in the rooms, though some will charge for their use.

• Many larger cities have numerous wireless (WiFi) 'hotspots', where the internet can be accessed by any computer with a standard wireless modem. Cards that allow access for a specific period (usually 24 hours) after activation can be bought at major hotels and some stores, which will also provide maps of nationwide coverage.

• Many public telephones that support international calls also have modem and DSL jacks, allowing a laptop to be connected using a modem cable and a regular phone card.

• Internet cafes are growing in number, but are somewhat different to those in the west. For a small fee – often around 200 yen per hour – customers can access the web on a computer in a small cubicle with a comfy chair or even a sofa. Most are open 24 hours a day, and offer other facilities including large libraries of comic books, rest rooms, shower stalls and free coffee. Many young people spend extended periods in these places and even sleep there, as they are the cheapest form of overnight accommodation in the country.

• Almost all public computers in Japan use Microsoft Windows® and Internet Explorer®. These will of course be in their Japanese versions, but as all the icons and shortcut keys are the same as in the western versions it is possible for non-Japanese readers to use them. Some public libraries also have computers available for public web access.

are there any internet cafés here?	この辺りにインターネットカフェはありますか
	kono atari ni intaanetto kafe wa arimasu ka?
how much is it to log on for an hour?	１時間いくらですか
	ichi-jikan ikura desu ka?
I want to check my e-mail	メールをチェックしたいです
	mēru o chekku shtai dess
I'd like to put these photos onto CD	写真をCDに入れたいです
	shashin o shīdī ni iretai dess
can you print it out?	プリントアウトをしてください
	purintoauto o shtekudasai?
can you help me please?	手伝ってくれませんか
	tetsudatte kuremasen ka?
this computer has crashed	コンピューターがクラッシュしました
	konpūta ga kurasshu shimashta

Practical info

Numbers

••

- You will see roman numerals used for prices, etc.
- Before contact with China (about 1500 years ago), Japan had no written language.
- Using numbers to count people and things is complicated, since they alter according to what is being counted.
- Keep pen and paper handy for writing down numbers.

The following are used for counting objects that have special counting particles; also as abstract numbers (eg. '1, 2, 3 go', etc.):

0	零	rei
1	一	ichi
2	二	ni
3	三	san
4	四	yon *or* shi
5	五	go
6	六	rok
7	七	shichi *or* nana
8	八	hachi
9	九	kyu *or* ku
10	十	ju

The following are used for counting objects that do not have special counting particles:

1	一つ	hitots
2	二つ	futats
3	三つ	mitts
4	四つ	yotts
5	五つ	itsuts
6	六つ	mutts
7	七つ	nanats
8	八つ	yatts
9	九つ	kokonots
10	十	tō
11	十一	jū-ichi
12	十二	jū-ni
13	十三	jū-san
14	十四	jū-yon *or* jū-shi
15	十五	jū-go
16	十六	jū-rok
17	十七	jū-nana
18	十八	jū-hachi
19	十九	jū-ku *or* jū-kyū
20	二十	ni-jū
21	二十一	ni-jū-ichi
22	二十二	ni-jū-ni
30	三十	san-jū
40	四十	yon-jū
50	五十	go-jū
60	六十	roku-jū
70	七十	nana-jū
80	八十	hachi-jū
90	九十	kyū-jū
100	百	hyak
110	百十	hyaku-ichi
200	二百	ni-hyak
300	三百	sam-byak
500	五百	go-hyak

1000	千	sen
2000	二千	ni-sen
10,000	一千	ichi-man
million	百万	hyaku-man

Days and months

- In Japanese, dates tend to be written in year, month, day form. So 17 August 2008 will be 2008.8.17.
- Months are literally, January = '1-month', February = '2-month', March = '3-month' and so on.
- Japan has four marked seasons: spring (March-May), when the cherry blossom is out; summer (June-August), when it gets very muggy; Autumn (Sep-Nov), usually dry with clear skies; and winter (Nov-Feb), which can be snowy on the mountains.

2008	2008年
	ni-sen hachi-nen
2009	2009年
	ni-sen kyu-nen
what is the date?	何日ですか
	kyō wa nan-nichi dess ka?
which day?	何日
	nan nichi?
which month?	何月
	nan gats?
March 5th	五月五日
	go gats itska
July 6th	六月六日
	roku gats muika
Saturday	土曜日
	doyōbi

on Saturdays	土曜日には
	doyōbi niwa
every Saturday	毎週土曜日
	maishū doyōbi
this Saturday	今週の土曜日
	konshu no doyōbi
next Saturday	来週の土曜日
	raishū no doyōbi
last Saturday	先週の土曜日
	senshū no doyōbi
please can you confirm the date	日にちを確認してください
	hinichi o kakunin shte kudasai

Monday	月曜日	getsu-yōbi
Tuesday	火曜日	ka-yōbi
Wednesday	水曜日	sui-yōbi
Thursday	木曜日	moku-yōbi
Friday	金曜日	kin-yōbi
Saturday	土曜日	do-yōbi
Sunday	日曜日	nichi-yōbi

January	一月	ichi-gats (1 month)
February	二月	ni-gats (2 month)
March	三月	san-gats (3 month)
April	四月	shi-gats (4 month)
May	五月	go-gats (5 month)
June	六月	roku-gats (6 month)
July	七月	shichi-gats (7 month)
August	八月	hachi-gats (8 month)
September	九月	ku-gats (9 month)
October	十月	jū-gats (10 month)
November	十一月	jū-ichi-gats (11 month)
December	十二月	jū-ni-gats (12 month)

Time

● Japan is 9 hours ahead of Greenwich Mean Time, 13 or 14 hours ahead of New York and Toronto and 1 hour behind Australia.
● Shops generally open 10am-8pm, seven days a week. Department stores close earlier on Sundays.
● Office hours are 9am-5pm, Monday-Friday.

what's the time?	何時ですか	
	nan-ji dess ka?	
am	午前	go-zen
pm	午後	go-go
1 o'clock	一時	ichi-ji
2 o'clock	二時	ni-ji
3 o'clock	三時	san-ji
4 o'clock	四時	yo-ji
5 o'clock	五時	go-ji
6 o'clock	六時	roku-ji
7 o'clock	七時	shichi-ji
8 o'clock	八時	hachi-ji
9 o'clock	九時	ku-ji
10 o'clock	十時	jū-ji
11 o'clock	十一時	ju-ichi-ji
12 o'clock	十二時	ju-ni-ji
(noon)	正午	sho-go
(midnight)	夜中	yo-naka
8.15	八時十五分	
	hachi-ji ju-go-fun	
8.30	八時半	
	hachi-ji han	

8.45	八時四十五分
	hachi-ji-yon-ju-go-fun
when?	いつ
	itsu?
at what time?	何時に
	nan-ji ni?
when do you open?	何時に開きますか
	nan-ji ni akimass ka?
at mid-day	正午に
	shōgo ni
when do you close?	何時に閉まりますか
	nan-ji ni shimemass ka?
at midnight	夜12時に
	yoru ju-ni-ji ni
it is one o'clock	一時です
	ichi-ji dess
it is three o'clock	三時です
	san-ji dess
we arrived early	早く着きました
	hayaku tsukimashta
we arrived late	遅れて着ました
	okurete tsukimashta
soon	間もなく
	mamonaku
later	あとで
	ato de

Holidays and festivals

• The traditional Japanese festival is called **matsuri**. **Shintō** belief is closely linked to the rice-growing cycle: prayers for a good harvest in the New Year, planting, harvesting and thanksgiving; while Buddhism places special importance on the remembrance of ancestors.

The return of their spirits each midsummer is celebrated in the country-wide summer festivals (**natsu matsuri**) and **Obon**. In the Tokyo area this takes place during the middle of July, while in other parts of the country it tends to be the middle of August. Apart from the national festivals, there are many local **matsuri**. Ask the TIC for information.

• Most public offices and many businesses are closed on national holidays. Shops are open (except for New Year). Public transport runs according to Sunday timetables but can be very crowded.

• If a national holiday falls on a Sunday, it's celebrated that day, but the Monday also becomes a holiday. Christmas isn't an official holiday.

1–3 January	New Year Families visit shrines, invite or visit friends or relatives
2nd Monday in January	Coming-of-age Day Ceremonies for young people who turn 20. **Kimono** are often worn
11 Februray	National Foundation Day
20–21 March	Spring Equinox
29 April–5 May	Golden Week
29 April	Green Day The birthday of **Emperor Shōwa**
3 May	Constitution Day
4 May	'Between Day' to bridge national holidays
5 May	Children's Day
3rd Monday in July	Marine Day
3rd Monday in September	Respect-for-the-aged Day
23–24 September	Autumn Equinox
2nd Monday in October	Health-Sports Day
3 November	Culture Day
23 November	Labour Thanksgiving Day
23 December	Emperor's Birthday

Eating out

Eating out

Traditional Japanese food consists of a few staple ingredients plus some side dishes. If necessary, food is cut into manageable bits before being served so that everything can be picked up easily with **hashi** (chopsticks). Try and practise with chopsticks before you arrive in Japan; it will increase your confidence. The word **gohan** means 'meal' as well as 'rice', which gives an idea of rice's importance.

Generally speaking, the eye stimulates the appetite in Japanese cuisine, whereas it is more the nose in western cooking. Furthermore, for many Japanese the concept of **hagotae**, (literally 'teeth-reponse') is very important, especially in the case of **gohan** (boiled rice). This is the feel (not so much the actual taste) which the food has inside the mouth. For westerners, the 'feel' of toast in the mouth, with its crunchy exterior and soft interior may be akin to Japanese fussiness about the 'right' rice or **tofu** (bean curd).

Japanese are generally eclectic in their food tastes, and separate them into **nihon–ryōri** (Japanese cuisine), **seiyō–ryōri** (western cuisine), **chūka–ryōri** (Chinese cuisine) and **kankoku–ryōri** (Korean cuisine). You're unlikely to find authentic-tasting international cuisine apart from in very expensive foreign restaurants with imported non-Japanese chefs. Japanese attempts at western food look very good, but can taste rather bland.

Breakfast is either western-style – ham and eggs, toast and coffee, etc., or Japanese-style, such as **gohan** (rice), into which a raw egg is stirred. Side dishes are **miso** soup (from soy beans), **nattō** (fermented soy beans), **tsukemono** (pickles) and **nori** (seaweed), washed down with **o-cha** (green tea). Lunch, eaten between 12 and 1, is often noodles or sandwiches. Lunchboxes, **o-bentō**, are popular. Dinner (around 6pm) is when families eat together (although fathers might not arrive until much later in the evening during the week).

Ordering drinks

• Cafés, which serve mostly non-alcoholic drinks and snacks, are a good place to relax as you can linger as long as you like.
• Cafés tend to be very smokey. Almost all are operated by chains such as Doutor and Starbucks.
• **O-cha** is green tea and is drunk throughout the day. It is drunk without milk and is usually free with your meal.
• **Kōcha** is black tea (what you are probably more used to).
• Traditional coffee shops (**kissaten**) can be very expensive. They are often used as business meeting places.

may I have a black coffee	コーヒーを下さい burak kōhī onegai shimass
may I have an American coffee *(not so strong)*	アメリカンコーヒーお願いします amerikan kōhī onegai shimass
may I have two cups of coffee	コーヒーを二つお願いします kōhī futats o onegai shimass
Indian tea	紅茶 kō-cha
green tea	お茶 ō-cha

may I have a tea with lemon	レモンティーお願いします
	remon kō–cha onegai shimass
may I have an iced coffee	アイスコーヒーお願いします
	aisu kōhī onegai shimass
may I have an iced tea	アイスティーお願いします
	aisu tee onegai shimass

• When out with Japanese, it is the custom to pour drinks for other people at your table. Don't pour your own drink – wait until someone does it for you.

• Brewery-run bars such as **Suntory**, **Asahi** and **Kirin** sell beer and food. These are generally not too expensive.

• If you are out with Japanese business associates, watch out for the amount you drink. An empty glass calls out to be replenished.

may I have some mineral water	ミネラルウオーターお願いします
	mineraru uōtā onegai shimass
sparkling	炭酸水
	tansansui
still	ミネラルウォーター
	mineraru uōtā
2 bottles please	二本お願いします
	ni–hon onegai shimass
do you have...?	...はありますか
	...wa arimass ka?
the wine list please	ワインのメニューを下さい
	wain no menyū o kudasai
a bottle of red wine	赤ワインを一本
	aka wain o ippon
a bottle of white wine	白ワインを一本
	shiro wain o ippon
a glass of ... wine	グラスワインの...
	guras wain no...

red	赤
	aka
white	白
	shiro
would you like a drink?	何か飲みませんか
	nani ka nomimasen ka?
what will you have?	何がよろしいですか
	nani ga yoroshī dess ka?
another round please	お代わりをお願いします
	o-kawari o onegai shimass
cheers!	乾杯!
	kanpai!
I've had enough thanks	もう結構です
	mo kekkō dess

Ordering food

- Restaurants close early, between 10 and 11pm.
- Noodle shops are a good place to eat a quick meal. It is worth learning the **kanji** for chicken, pork and beef.
- Most Japanese restaurants will bring you chopsticks, but knife, fork and spoon are available on request.
- Never leave chopsticks sticking in food, especially rice (it is a symbol of death).
- In some restaurants which use **tatami** you have to remove shoes.

may I/we enter?	入ってもいいですか
	haitte mo ī dess ka?
do you serve meals?	食事はできますか
	shoku-ji wa dekimass ka?
a table for ... please	...のテーブルをお願いします
	...no tēburu o onegai shimass

one/2/3	一人用/二人用/三人用
	hitori-yō/futari-yō/san-nin-yō
please show me the menu	メニューを見せてください
	menyū o misete kudasai
do you have a menu in English?	英語のメニューはありますか
	eigo no menyū wa arimass ka?
I'd like the set meal	定食を下さい
	teishok o kudasai
the assorted set please (e.g. in the case of sushi)	盛り合わせを下さい
	moriawase o kudasai

• Most restaurants automatically bring a glass of tap water (which is safe to drink) and a small hand towel (**oshibori**).
• Most restaurants offer a cheap **setto** (set meal) at lunchtime, but portions tend to be small.
• In most local cafés you can get breakfast for about the price of a cup of coffee. Ask for a morning set – **morningu setto kudasai**. Bread is **pan**, toast is **tōsto**, salad is **o-sarada** and fruit is **o-kudamono**.

what do you recommend?	何がお勧めですか
	nani ga o-susume dess ka?
please choose for me	お任せします
	o-makase shimass
I'll have this	これを下さい
	kore o kudasai
I don't eat meat	肉は食べません
	niku wa tabemasen
some more of ... please	...をもう少し下さい
	...o mō skoshi kudasai
do you have any vegetarian dishes?	ベジタリアン料理はありますか
	bejitarian ryōri wa arimass ka?

excuse me!	すみません!
	sumimasen!
some water please	パンを下さい
	o-mizu o kudasai
a knife and fork please	ナイフとフォークを下さい
	naifu to fōku o kudasai
bon appetit!	いただきます!
	itadakimass!
thanks for the delicious meal	ごちそうさまでした
	go-chisō-sama deshta
the bill please	お勘定をお願いします
	o-kanjō o onegai shimass
shall we go Dutch?	割勘でいいですか
	warikan de ī dess ka?

Special requirements

• •

- There are very few vegetarian restaurants in Japan.
- Many restaurants have very limited selections of vegetarian dishes.
- Fruit can be rather expensive.
- Many Japanese dishes include raw fish. For this reason the fish has to be extremely fresh.

what is this?	これは何ですか
	kore wa nan dess ka?
I'm vegetarian	ベジタリアンです
	bejitarian dess
I don't eat fish	魚は食べません
	sakana wa tabemasen
I don't eat pork	豚肉は食べません
	buta-nik wa tabemasen
I'm allergic to shellfish	私は貝にアレルギーがあります
	watashi wa kai ni arerugī ga arimass

I am allergic to peanuts	私はピーナッツにアレルギーがあります
	watashi wa pīnats ni arerugi ga arimass
I can't eat raw eggs	生卵は食べません
	nama tamago wa tabemasen
is it raw?	それは生ですか
	sore wa nama dess ka?
I'm on a diet	ダイエット中です
	daietto chu des
I don't drink alcohol	アルコールは飲みません
	arukōru wa nomimasen

Eating photoguide

Eating places

Food In Japan You can find all types of eating places and foods in Japan. US-style fast food is popular. Visit **www.japan-guide.com** for an overview. And **www.bento.com** for a guide to eating out in Japan.

Traditional Japanese restaurants have low tables and **tatami** matting. You have to remove your shoes so make sure your socks are respectable.

Traditional Tea House The less garish the establishment, the more traditional (and probably more expensive) it will be.

A 10% service charge is generally included in the bill and there is no tipping. The word for 'the bill' or 'check' is **kanjō**.

Eating places

Traditional Coffee Shops – known as **kissaten** (serving mostly non-alcoholic drinks and snacks) are good places to relax as you can linger for as long as you like. The only problem is that they can become very smokey. Most coffee shops and restaurants will automatically bring you a glass of tap water (which is safe to drink) and a small hand towel to wipe your face and hands.

Kissaten are popular meeting places to do business.

Tea Ordinary tea (not green tea) is **kōcha**. Green tea is **ocha** and is usually drunk with Japanese meals. You generally don't have milk in it.

Bakery Western-style bakeries abound. Japanese patisserie tends to be heavier on salt and sugar and uses a lot of artificial flavoured cream. French bread is very good and baked fresh every morning

Convenience Stores If you need a late-night snack, or don't want the hassle of going to a restaurant, you can buy microwaveable snacks (such as pot noodles) in convenience stores. Try acquiring a taste for rice balls (which you can buy at any convenience store). They can become addictive and filling. Basements of department stores are good places for food, but they can be expensive!

Vending Machines have all kinds of hot and cold snacks.

Sashimi is slices of raw fish. **Sushi** is fish on rice. Men eat **sushi** after work rather like Spanish people eat tapas. Look out for the conveyor belt **sushi** (**kaitenzushi**), where the price is shown by the colour of the plate.

Breakfasts In most local cafes you can get breakfast for about the price of a cup of coffee. Ask for a morning set (**morningu setto, kudasai**). You will be given some choices. Ask for **kōhī** (coffee), **kōcha** (black tea), **o-sarada** for salad and **o-kudamono** for fruit. **Pan** is bread and **tosto** is toast.

Department Stores
Most department stores have a selection of eating places on different floors. **Raion** 'Lion' is one of the many popular chains of eateries.

Lunchtime Most restaurants offer a cheap **setto** (set meal) at lunchtime, but portions tend to be rather small. Lunch on this menu board is from 10am–3pm. You can buy pre-packed **o-bentō** (lunch-boxes) in most supermarkets, station kiosks, etc. There are also shops selling **hoka hoka bentō** (hot lunchboxes).

Fast food addicts can always find a fix in Japan.

Plastic Food Many eating places in Japan have plates of plastic food on display to show customers what they offer. When out with Japanese, it is the custom to pour drinks for other people at your table. Don't pour your own drink, wait until somebody does it for you. Take care if you drink quite quickly, you may find your glass being refilled more often than you would like.

Noodle Shop Noodles are Japanese fast food. People are very helpful in noodle shops. Popular choices are chicken – **toriniku** and beef – **gyuniku**. It is worth learning the **kanji** characters for these so that you can spot them in a menu.

Beer Chain Beer (similar to German lager) is popular and often drunk with meals. The big breweries include **Suntory**, **Asahi** and **Kirin**. They own chains of pub-type restaurants such as Lion's Beer Hall and Kirin City – good places for inexpensive food. Women can feel quite at ease there. The word for cheers is **kanpai!** Bon appétit is **itadakimass!**

Fish Markets There are markets selling most foods in Japan – from the fish markets in coastal cities which open in the early hours of the morning to stalls selling an assortment of sour pickles. It is worth trying to visit the fish market in Tokyo (**Tsukiji**) and sampling the **sushi** at one of the **sushi** counters. (They tend to look like dives, but don't be put off, ask around to find out which one is the best.) They often have a 2-option selection – one is around ¥2,500 and the other is ¥3,000. If you are an adventurous eater, go for the more expensive option, you'll taste fish you have never experienced elsewhere. Otherwise, if you just want to try some wonderful **sushi**, stick with the first option.

Izakaya This is an eatery and bar. The white curtain hung outside the door indicates that it is open for business. If the door is open but the curtain is inside, they aren't open yet.

Restaurants close quite early – between 10–11pm.

Restaurants Most restaurants have the menu and prices displayed outside. Many menus are also picture menus which means that you can see exactly what you are going to order.

Noodle Shop Menu

Different Cuisines Japanese like a wide range of different foods and separate them into **nihon-ryōri** (Japanese cuisine), **seiyo-ryōri** (western cuisine), **chūka-ryōri** (Chinese cuisine) and **kankoku-ryōri** (Korean cuisine).

Spanish Restaurant

Italian Restaurant
Japanese food has some subtle flavours, little fat and a relatively high salt content.

Italian Menu

Seafood

Chinese Restaurant

Korean Barbecue Restaurant

Yakitori These restaurants serve grilled chicken on skewers. They are usually lively places which are frequented by business men after work. Check at the restaurant entrance what credit cards are accepted. Outside main cities you may find it more difficult to find places that have the facility to accept credit cards.

Tempura is seafood and vegetables deep fried in **tempura** batter. It was originally brought to Japan by the Portuguese. Good **tempura** can be expensive.

Japanese Restaurants Most Japanese restaurants will automatically bring chopsticks (**hashi**), but knives and forks are available on request. **Sushi** bars can be quite intimidating. There is often no menu on the outside and you cannot see into most of them. Prices can vary enormously and it is hard to tell if you are going into a super-expensive one. If the first price on the menu is around ¥200, then the place won't bankrupt you. Tea (**o-cha**) automatically comes free as does the pickled ginger (**gari**).

Restaurants outside the cities In this traditional country restaurant the food is cooked over charcoal.

Raw fish is a delicacy in Japan. A freshly-killed fish might still twitch after death. Japanese see this as an indication of how fresh the fish is.

Sake is warmed in freshly-cut bamboo, giving it a wonderful aroma.

Green wasabi Japanese horseradish can be breathtakingly hot. Be careful!

Try telling your hosts that you love Japanese food, except for **nattō** (fermented beans eaten at breakfast). You either love **nattō** or hate it. This should convince your host that you know enough about Japanese food to order dishes for you, rather than steering you towards western restaurants. Say **oishī**, after the first mouthful to show your appreciation.

Eating places

All types of eating places and food can be found in Japan. Except in hotel restaurants and up-market traditional Japanese restaurants, which usually have set dining times, you can have your meal at any time throughout the day. American style fast food is popular. There are also many specialized restaurants where only one type of food is served, for example, **Soba-ya** (Japanese noodle shop), **Rāmen-ya** (Chinese noodle shop), **Sushi-ya** (Sushi restaurant), **Tonkatsu-ya** (pork cutlet restaurant) and even **Unagi** (BBQ eel restaurant). Visit **www.bento.com** for a guide to eating out in Japan.

Most coffee shops and restaurants will automatically bring you a glass of tap water (which is safe to drink) and **Oshibori**, a small hand towel to wipe your hands. In traditional Japanese restaurants you will find low tables and (often) **tatami matting** which is a traditional Japanese mat made of straw. These restaurants require you to remove your shoes, so make sure your socks are respectable. Many eating places in Japan have plates of plastic food on display to show customers what they offer.

Coffee shops 喫茶店 (kissaten)

Coffee shops serve non-alcoholic drinks and many of them also serve foods such as salads, sandwiches, pasta dishes and rice dishes. It is fun to find a good morning service which includes a small complementary breakfast when you order a coffee or tea, usually up to 10 or 11am. Ask for **mōningu setto**. If you would like to order tea with milk, be sure to specify **miruku tī**, as otherwise you will probably be served a lemon tea.

Noodle shops
蕎麦屋 (soba-ya)　うどん屋 (udon-ya)　ラーメン屋 (rāmen-ya)

Noodles are Japanese fast food. There are three popular types of noodles in Japan. These are **soba**, **udon** and **rāmen**. **Soba** (buckwheat noodles) and **udon** (white flour noodles) are both traditional Japanese noodles. You can choose different toppings such as chicken or tempura. **Rāmen** originated from China but has gained huge popularity amongst all generations in Japan. It comes in hot soup or is served cold without soup, in summer.

Sushi shops 鮨屋 (sushi-ya)

There are a number of different **sushi** types but the most popular are **nigiri-zushi**, (a rice ball shaped in the palm of the hand with raw fish on top), and **temaki-zushi**, (rice and raw fish often wrapped in a cone shape with a seaweed sheet wrapper). **Toro**, a special part of tuna, is also very popular. Although generally **sushi** is expensive, you can find good deals at lunch time or at very cheap and decent quality 'rotating' (**kaiten**) **sushi** shops where the **sushi** passes by on a conveyor belt, and you can pick what you fancy. One plate usually costs about 200 yen.

Tempura shops 天麩羅屋 (tempura-ya)

Tempura is a deep fried dish of vegetables and seafood in light batter. It was originally introduced by the Portuguese.

Family restaurants ファミリーレストラン (famirī resutoran)

There are many chain family restaurants located on major roads. Resembling American diners, with waitress service and kids' menus.

Pubs 居酒屋 (izaka-ya)

Izaka-ya are good places to try a range of Japanese food and drink. They serve cheap but tasty food in small portions similar to Spanish tapas, and usually have a large selection to choose from. Try, **Yakitori** (BBQ chicken), **Agedashi-dofu** (deep-fried bean curd) and **Sashimi** (sliced raw fish).

Convenience stores コンビニ (konbini)

If you need a late-night snack or don't want to go to a restaurant, a convenience store is a good place to stock up on snacks. Sandwiches, salads, pot noodles, etc. are all available to buy, as well as rice balls, which have various fillings and can become addictive.

Department stores デパート (depāto)

Most department stores have a designated restaurant floor (usually on the top floor) where you will find various types of restaurant, including western style. These are good places to visit to familiarize yourself with the kind of food you can get in Japan, but are not cheap. Basement floors have good but expensive delis and take-away food.

Lunch boxes お弁当 (obentō)

Obentō is a pre-packed lunchbox. You can buy various types from department stores, convenience stores, supermarkets and even train stations. Each train station sells specialized lunchboxes prepared with local delicacies such as dimsum lunchbox in Yokohama, Tempura riceball in Nagoya, BBQ eel in Hamamatsu and Trout sushi in Toyama.

Vending machines 自動販売機 (jidō-hanbaiki)

Vending machines contain all kinds of drinks and snacks.

Drinks to try

Iced coffee アイスコーヒー **aisukōhī** is very popular in Japan.

Japanese tea お茶 **ocha** is usually served with your meal for free in Japanese restaurants including Japanese noodle shops. You can buy chilled or hot canned tea from vending machines. There are many kinds to choose from.

Green tea 抹茶 **maccha**/グリーンティー **gurīn tī** is the tea used at tea ceremonies and is rather bitter, but a sweet iced green tea is available in some coffee shops. Green tea ice cream is a popular favourite.

Japanese rice wine 酒 **sake** can be drunk either chilled or warmed. There are different degrees of sweetness and lots of local ones, which are called 地酒 **jizake**.

焼酎 **Shōchū** is Japanese vodka. It is cheap and again there are many local varieties.

チュウハイ **Chūhai** is a mixture of **shōchū** and lemonade, etc. which is popular among young people.

梅酒 **Umeshu** is Japanese plum wine. It is smooth and sweet and many women are fond of it.

Service charge/tax and tip

A consumer tax of 5% and a service charge of 10% are generally included in the bill and there is no tipping.

Bill

The word for the bill is **(O)kanjō**. You can ask for the bill by saying '(O)kanjō onegai shimass'.

Menu reader

Although traditional Japanese cuisine, **kaiseki-ryōri**, has a long list of dishes (which is usually a set course), most Japanese restaurants, unlike western restaurants, do not have separate starters or main meals. Here are sample menus for various popular eating places.

Table top cooking restaurant

鉄板焼き **teppan-yaki** meat, seafood and vegetables cooked on a table-top hot plate

すき焼き **suki-yaki** sliced beef, bean curd, mushroom and other vegetables cooked in a soy sauce based sauce

しゃぶしゃぶ **shabu-shabu** thinly sliced beef dipped and cooked quickly in a hot stock, eaten with sesame seed, soy sauce and Japanese lime based dip

General Japanese and Izaka-ya restaurants

Japanese restaurants often have a set meal (定食 **teishoku**), which is a main dish with a bowl of rice, soup, and a side dish all served together on a tray. **Izaka-ya** normally serve food in small portions.

Beef 牛肉 (gyū-niku)

牛丼 **gyū-don** sliced beef cooked with soy sauce on rice

牛肉たたき **gyū-niku tataki** seared sliced beef served with ginger

牛刺し **gyū-sashi** sliced raw beef

ハンバーグ **hambāgu** hamburger steak

ハンバーガー **hambāgā** hamburger

串かつ **kushi-katsu** crumbled meat and vegetables, deep-fried on skewers

肉じゃが nikujaga sliced beef cooked with potato in a soy sauce stock
レバー rebā grilled or pan-fried liver
しゃぶしゃぶ shabushabu thinly sliced beef cooked quickly at the table in boiling stock
すきやき suki-yaki sliced beef with vegetables and raw egg, cooked at the table
ステーキ sutēki steak
焼き肉 yaki-niku grilled sliced beef

Chicken 鶏肉 (tori-niku)

から揚げ kara-age deep-fried chicken coated in mild spice and herbs
ねぎま negima char-grilled skewered chicken and spring onion
竜田揚げ tatta-age deep-fried marinated (soy sauce, sake, ginger) chicken
照り焼きチキン teriyaki-chikin pan-fried chicken in teriyaki-sauce (soy sauce and rice wine)
つくね tsukune minced chicken ball char-grilled and coated with soy sauce
焼き鳥 yaki-tori char-grilled skewered chicken

Pork 豚肉 (buta-niku)

豚肉の生姜焼き buta-niku no shōga yaki pan-fried thinly sliced pork with soy sauce and ginger
餃子 gyōza fried pork dumpling
かつ丼 katsudon deep-fried, bread-crumbed pork cutlet on rice
かつカレー katsu-karē deep-fried, bread-crumbed pork and curry on rice
とんかつ tonkatsu deep-fried, bread-crumbed pork cutlet
焼き豚/チャーシュー yakibuta/chāshū sliced roast pork

Fish 魚 (sakana) and other seafood dishes

See type of fish in the Sushi shop section below.

刺身 **sashimi** sliced raw fish
焼き魚 **yaki-zakana** grilled fish
煮魚 **ni-zakana** simmered fish
エビフライ **ebi-furai** deep-fried, crumbed shrimp
えび天ぷら **ebi-tempura** deep-fried shrimp in light batter topped on rice
かきフライ **kaki-furai** deep-fried, crumbed oyster
かにすき **kanisuki** hotpot dish with crabs
かに酢（の物）**kanisu (nomono)** crab meat in white rice vinegar
かつおたたき **katsuo tataki** seared bonito with grated ginger
いかの姿焼き **ika no sugata-yaki** whole grilled squid
いわしの生姜煮 **iwashi no shōga-ni** simmered gingered sardine
さばの塩焼き **saba no shioyaki** salt-grilled mackerel
さばの味噌煮 **saba no misoni** simmered mackerel in miso sauce
さばの竜田揚げ **saba no tatta-age** deep-fried marinated (soy sauce, sake, ginger) mackerel
さんまの塩焼き **samma no shioyaki** salt-grilled (Pacific) saury
酢牡蛎 **sugaki** fresh oyster in vinegar
刺身盛り合わせ **sashimi moriawase** assorted sliced raw fish
たこ焼き **takoyaki** octopus cooked in a dough ball
たら **tara** cod
たらの味噌焼き **tara no miso yaki** grilled cod with soy bean paste
てっさ **tessa** thinly sliced raw puffer fish (prepared by a licensed chef)
うな重 **unajū**／うな丼 **unadon** grilled eel on rice

Vegetables 野菜 (yasai)

揚げだし豆腐 **agedashi-dōfu** deep-fried bean curd
ふろふきだいこん **furoruki daikon** simmered Japanese radish with sauce

冷奴 **hiyayakko** cold bean curd

ほうれん草おひたし **hōrensō ohitashi** cooked spinach with sesame seeds

かぼちゃの煮物 **kabocha no nimono** simmered pumpkin

きんぴらごぼう **kimpira gobō** shaved burdock root, pan-fried with soy sauce and chilli

きのこ **kinoko** various mushrooms

こんにゃく **konnyaku** firm, jelly made from arrowroot

きゅうりの酢の物 **kyūri no suno mono** sliced cucumber in vinegar

のり **nori** dried seaweed sheet

納豆 **nattō** fermented soy beans

ポテトフライ **poteto furai** French fries

白和え **shira-ae** boiled vegetables mixed with bean curd

漬物 **tsukemono** pickled vegetables

わかめの酢の物 **wakame no suno mono** seaweed in vinegar

焼きなす **yakinasu** grilled aubergine

焼きしいたけ **yaki-shītake** grilled Japanese **shītake**-mushroom

野菜天ぷら **yasai tempura** deep-fried vegetables in light batter

Rice ご飯 (gohan) and others

おでん **oden** various vegetables, bean curd and skewered beef tendon cooked in stock

お好み焼き **okonomi-yaki** Japanese style pizza (see more in **Okonomi-yaki** shop section)

そば **soba** thin, brown, buckwheat noodles

うどん **udon** thick, white, wheat flour noodles

ラーメン **rāmen** Chinese style noodles (see more in noodle shop section)

カレー **karē** curry and rice

かつカレー **katsu-karē** bread-crumbed, deep-fried pork on curry and rice

かつ丼 **katsu-don** crumbed, deep-fried pork, egg and onion cooked
with soy sauce on rice

天丼 **tendon** deep-fried prawn in light batter on rice

牛丼 **gyūdon** sliced beef, onion and egg cooked with soy sauce on rice

スパゲティー **supagetī** spaghetti

ピザ **piza** pizza

雑炊 **zōsui** Japanese savoury rice porridge with egg

鮭茶漬け **sake-chazuke** Japanese tea poured over rice, flaked salmon
and seaweed

お茶漬け **o-chazuke** Japanese tea poured over rice

おにぎり **onigiri** rice ball wrapped with seaweed sheet

焼き飯 **yakimeshi** Japanese style fried rice

チャーハン **chāhan** Chinese style fried rice

だし巻き卵 **dashimaki tamago** rolled flavoured eggs

Soup 汁 (shiru)

豆腐の味噌汁 **tōfu no misoshiru** soy bean paste based soup with
soy bean curd

わかめの味噌汁 **wakame no misoshiru** soy bean paste based soup
with seaweed

ねぎの味噌汁 **negi no misoshiru** soy bean paste based soup with
spring onion

あげの味噌汁 **age no misoshiru** soy bean paste based soup with
bean curd sheet

雑煮 **zōni** soup with rice cake

すまし汁 **sumashijiru** clear soup

Drinks お飲み物 (o-nomimono)

ビール **bīru** lager beer

生ビール **nama bīru** draft beer

瓶ビール **bin-bīru** bottled beer

大ジョッキ dai-jokki　large glass of lager
中ジョッキ chū-jokki　medium glass of lager
小ジョッキ shō-jokki　small glass of lager
酒 sake　Japanese rice wine, warm or chilled
チュウハイ chūhai　Japanese vodka with lemonade
水割り mizu-wari　whisky with water
コーラ kōra　cola
ジュース jūsu　juice
オレンジジュース orenji-jūsu　orange juice
お茶 o-cha　Japanese tea. Traditionally in a sushi shop, tea is served
　　after you finish the meal. This tea is called あがり agari.
水 mizu　water
炭酸水 tansansui　sparkling water
ミネラルウォーター mineraru uōtā　mineral water (still)
コーヒー kōhī　coffee
紅茶 kōcha　English tea

Sushi shop

Sushi normally means rice balls (**nigiri**) with sliced raw fish but
there are various types.

にぎり(鮨) nigiri (zushi)　rice balls with sliced raw fish
手巻き寿司 temaki-zushi　rolled sushi with seaweed sheet (without
　　using bamboo sheet)
巻き寿司 maki-zushi　rolled sushi with seaweed sheet using bamboo
　　sheet
細巻き hoso-maki　small rolled sushi
太巻き futo-maki　large rolled sushi with cooked egg, vegetable,
　　mushroom, etc. usually vegetarian
いなり寿司 inari-zushi　seasoned rice, wrapped in fried thin bean
　　curd
カッパ (巻き) kappa (maki)　small rolled sushi with cucumber
盛り合わせ moriawase　assorted sushi

For **nigiri** and **temaki**, you can choose what to put on/in from below:

あまえび **amaebi** sweet shrimps
赤貝 **akagai** ark shell (red shellfish)
穴子 **anago** conger eel (usually grilled)
あわび **awabi** abalone
えび **ebi** prawn
貝 **kai** shellfish
かに **kani** crab
かつお **katsuo** bonito
ひらめ **hirame** plaice
ホタテ **hotate** scallop
いか **ika** squid
いくら **ikura** salmon roe
いわし **iwashi** sardine
まぐろ **maguro** tuna
さば **saba** mackerel
鯛 **tai** snapper
たこ **tako** octopus
うなぎ **unagi** eel (usually grilled)
うに **uni** sea urchin
卵 **tamago** sliced, flavoured egg omelette

Soups and others

味噌汁 **misoshiru** soy bean paste based soup
すまし汁 **sumashi-jiru** clear soup
茶碗蒸し **chawan-mushi** steamed flavoured egg with vegetable,
    chicken, mushroom and prawn
わさび **wasabi** Japanese green horseradish
がり **gari** thinly sliced, pickled ginger

Noodle shop

そば **soba** thin, brown, buckwheat noodles
うどん **udon** thick, white, wheat flour noodles
そうめん **sō-men** thin, white, wheat flour cold noodles
ラーメン **raamen** Chinese style noodles

Udon and Soba

釜揚げうどん **kama-age udon** warm/cold udon with dipping sauce
カレーうどん/そば **karē udon/soba** udon/soba in curry soup
きつねうどん **kitsune udon** udon with flavoured bean curd sheet
木の葉うどん/そば **konoha udon/soba** udon/soba in soup with
sliced fish paste
鍋焼きうどん **nabeyaki udon** udon cooked in a clay pot with
vegetables, chicken, prawn, etc.
肉うどん/そば **niku udon/soba** udon/soba in soup with sliced beef
山菜うどん/そば **sansai udon/soba** udon/soba in soup with wild
vegetables
たぬきうどん/そば **tanuki udon/soba** udon/soba in soup with
deep-fried light batter
天ぷらうどん/そば **tempura udon/soba** udon/soba in soup with
deep-fried prawn in light batter
天ざる **tenzaru** cold soba and deep-fried prawn in light batter with
dipping sauce
ニシンそば **nishin soba** soba in soup with smoked herring
わかめうどん/そば **wakame udon/soba** udon/soba in soup with
seaweed
ざるそば **zaru soba** cold soba with dipping sauce

Rāmen: use chilli powder for **miso rāmen** but pepper (**koshō**) for
others.

味噌ラーメン miso rāmen rāmen in soy bean paste based soup

塩ラーメン shio rāmen rāmen in salt based soup

醤油ラーメン shooyu rāmen rāmen in soy sauce based soup

チャーシュー chaashuu rāmen in soy sauce based soup with an extra topping of sliced roast pork

チャンポン麺 champon-men rāmen in pork stock based soup with stir-fry meat and vegetables

コーンラーメン koon rāmen rāmen with sweetcorn

もやしラーメン moyashi rāmen rāmen with extra bean sprout topping

とんこつラーメン tonkotsu rāmen rāmen in pork stock based soup

Rice dishes and others

チャーハン chāhan Chinese style fried rice

えび天丼 ebi-tendon deep-fried prawn in light batter on rice

いなり寿司 inari-zushi seasoned rice, wrapped in fried thin bean curd

カレーライス karē raisu curry with rice

おにぎり onigiri rice ball wrapped with seaweed sheet

親子丼 oyako-don (buri) chicken and egg topped on rice

天ぷら tempura deep-fried seafood and vegetables in light batter

天丼 tendon deep-fried vegetables and prawn in light batter topped on rice

うどん/そば定食 udon/soba teishoku set meal with udon/soba, rice and side dish

焼き飯 yaki-meshi Japanese style fried rice

焼きうどん/そば yaki udon/soba udon/soba stir-fry with meat and vegetables

餃子 gyōza fried pork dumpling

Okonomi-yaki shop

お好み焼き **okonomi-yaki** Japanese style pizza, sliced cabbage and meat or seafood cooked in soft dough on a hot plate

焼きそば **yakisoba** stir-fried Chinese noodles with meat and vegetables

焼きうどん **yakiudon** stir-fried thick white flour noodles with meat and vegetables

モダン焼き **modan-yaki** yakisoba in thin flour crêpe

広島焼き **Hiroshima-yaki** Hiroshima style, ingredients covered with a thin flour crêpe instead of mixing them with dough

おにぎり **onigiri** rice ball

You can choose what to put in from the following:

牛肉 **gyū-niku** beef

豚肉 **buta-niku** pork

えび **ebi** shrimps

いか **ika** squid

たこ **tako** octopus

野菜 **yasai** vegetables (**yasai-yaki** is without any meat/seafood)

ねぎ **negi** spring onion (**negi-yaki** uses spring onion instead of cabbage)

卵/玉子 **tamago** egg

Possible vegetarian dishes

While vegetarian choices are occasionally found on menus, those averse to meat and animal products should be careful in Japan. Many Japanese would forget, for example, that the stock for their otherwise vegetarian soups is made from fish, or that they are using animal gelatin. Vegans, in particular, will find their choices limited when they go to eat out. Some cities have specialist vegetarian and vegan restaurants, however, and major Buddhist temples that accommodate foreigners, such as those at Koya-san near Osaka, keep a strictly vegetarian regime.

山菜料理 **sansai ryōri** Japanese vegetarian dish which could be a full course meal

おひたし **ohitashi** Japanese salad (steamed spinach or beans, etc. with sesame seeds)

豆腐 **toofu** bean curd (very popular)

冷奴 **hiyayakko** chilled tofu

卵丼 **tamago domburi** rice with cooked egg and vegetables (onions) in a soy sauce based sauce

巻き寿司 **maki-zushi** rolled sushi with mixed ingredients. You can also try カッパ巻き **kappamaki** (cucumber rolls) or 卵巻き **tamagomaki** (egg rolls)

わかめうどん/蕎麦 **wakame udon/soba** served with seaweed

ざるそば **zaru soba** chilled soba with dipping sauce

野菜お好み焼き **yasai okonomiyaki** Japanese style pizza with sliced cabbage, spring onion and egg, prepared on a hot plate

野菜天ぷら **yasai tempura** deep-fried vegetables in light batter

Grammar

Introduction

This is a guide to some basic concepts and rules in Japanese.
It is designed to enable you to make simple sentences and ask
questions, using a mode of address appropriate for a foreigner
travelling in Japan. Japanese grammar is remarkably simple
compared to that of most European languages, and the following
section contains everything necessary for survival conversation.

Word order

The basic word order of Japanese is subject-object-verb. The
relationships between words in a sentence are shown by placing
particles (so-called postpositions) behind the word which they control.
The main ones are ga (clause subject), wa (roughly translated
'as-for'), o (after the direct object), no (usually meaning 'of' in
English), and ka (showing that the preceding phrase is a question).

Plurals

Japanese has no plural forms and thus no articles like the English 'a',
'an' or 'the'. Unless it is absolutely necessary to define how many
are present, the number of things is left undefined. For example,
the word inu means 'dog', 'dogs' and 'the dogs'.

Personal pronouns

These are often omitted, but can be used where it would not otherwise be clear who the subject or object was:

Watashi	I, me
Anata	You (singular)

Note: there are a large number of terms for 'you', of varying politeness. If you know the other person's name, you should use it instead of 'you', with -san attached, even though this sounds as though you are talking about a third person.

Kare	He, him
Kanojo	She, her
Watash'tachi	We, us
Anatatachi	You (plural)
Karera	They

How to use verbs

Note: Japanese can be deliberately spoken at an enhanced level of politeness, which is contrived by the use of special verbs and the addition of prefixes to nouns. The beginner need not be concerned with this, however, as verbs in their normal form are considered perfectly appropriate for a foreigner starting out in the language. Here we explain how to use verbs in their normal form.

To use a verb, you first need to find its 'stem'. You do this by removing the ending from the 'infinitive' form (the form found in dictionaries, including this one) using the guide below. Then you add to the stem an ending that reflects your intended meaning.

For example: the verb wakaru (to understand) is one of the large group whose dictionary form ends with -ru. To make the stem, just change the -ru to -ri. Then add an ending:

wakari-mass	I, you, he, she, it, we or they **understand**.
wakari-mashta	I, you, he, she, it, we or they **understood**.
wakari-tai dess	I, you, he, she, it, we or they want/ wants to **understand**.

As you can see, there are no separate endings depending on who is the subject (such as 'I understand' but 'he understand<u>s</u>'), and concepts like 'want to' are simply expressed as forms of the verb. The main groups of verbs and the method for making their stems are:

Dictionary form ends with -ku, e.g. kaku: change the -ku to -ki.
Kakimass, kakimashta (write, wrote)

Dictionary form ends with -ru, e.g. wakaru: change the -ru to -ri.
Wakarimass, wakarimashta (understand, understood)

Dictionary form ends with -mu, e.g. nomu: change the -mu to -mi.
Nomimass, nomimashta (drink, drank)

Dictionary form ends with -u, e.g. kau: change the -u to -i.
Kaimass, kaitai dess (buy, want to buy)

Dictionary form ends with -su, e.g. hanasu: change the -su to -shi.
Hanashimass, hanashimashta (speak, spoke)

Dictionary form ends with -tsu, e.g. motsu: change the -tsu to -chi.
Mochimass, mochitai dess (carry, want to carry)

Dictionary form ends with -bu, e.g. yobu: change the -bu to -bi.
Yobimass, yobimashta (call, called)

Irregular verbs

. . . .

There are very few irregular verbs in Japanese. Unfortunately, they
are all ones you will need. One of them is 'to be', which has
no infinitive form:

dess am, are, is
watashi wa samui dess I am cold (literally: I – cold – am)

deshta was
kare wa shinsets deshta He was kind (he – kind – was)

dewa arimasen am, are, is not
watashi wa Amerika-jin dewa arimasen I am not an American

dewa arimasen deshta was not
ī eiga dewa arimasen deshta It/that was not a good movie
  ('ja' is often used instead of 'dewa')

Some verbs look like –ru verbs in their dictionary form, but behave
differently. One is suru, 'to do':

shimass do
kakunin shimass confirm (literally: confirmation – do)

shimashta did
nani o shimashta ka What did you do? (what – did – ka for question)

Another is kuru, 'to come':

kimass come
fuyu ga kimass Winter comes

kimashta came
kino kimashta They/we etc. came yesterday (**kino**: yesterday)

kite kudasai please come
koko ni kite kudasai Please come here

Several of these false -ru verbs behave in the same way. Their dictionary forms end in -iru, and their stem is made by simply removing the -ru and adding nothing. One is iru, to be present (for living, animate things):

imass is present
Kanojo wa imass She is here/there

imashta was present
Kare wa imashta He was here/there

Another is miru, 'to see, watch or look at':

mimass see
Eiga o mimass I/you etc. watch (a) movie(s)

mimashta saw
Kare o mimashta I/you etc. saw him

mite kudasai please look
Kore o mite kudasai Please look at this

And a third is dekiru, 'to be able to':

dekimass can
kore ga dekimass (I) can (do) this (literally: 'this – can')

dekimashta could, was able to
miru koto ga dekimashta I was able to see

Note: you can say 'I can...' by simply adding - koto ga dekimass
to the dictionary form of any verb:

Aruku koto ga dekimass I can walk
kiku koto ga dekimass I can hear

Negatives

To make the negative form, simply add -masen to the stem:

mimasen don't see
wakarimasen don't understand (from wakaru, to understand)
dekimasen cannot

For the negative form in the past tense, add -masen deshta:

mimasen deshta didn't see
wakarimasen deshta didn't understand
dekimasen deshta could not

The k-s-a rule

In Japanese, the concept of space is divided into three zones:
the space immediately around you (k), the space immediately
around the person to whom you are talking (s), and all other space,
including other times (a). Japanese articles and other words reflect
this division:

kore	this one
sore	that one (by the person to whom you are talking)
are	that one (over there, not near either of you)

kono hon	this book
sono hon	that book (the one the other person is holding, or that is next to them)
ano hon	that book (the one over there, or that book I read)

koko ni	here
soko ni	there (by the person to whom you are talking)
asoko ni	over there (away from either of you)

Here are some sample sentences that illustrate Japanese word order, particles, articles and verb forms:

Ashta wa doyobi dess. Tomorrow is Saturday (tomorrow – Saturday – is)

Ashta: tomorrow, plus **wa** to show that it's the subject of the sentence. You could use **kyo** (today) or **asatte** (the day after tomorrow) instead; if you use **kino** (yesterday), however, then **dess** changes to **deshta** (was): **kino wa doyobi deshta.**

Watashi wa ano eiga o mimashta. I saw that movie (I – that movie – saw)

Watashi is I; **wa** shows that I am the subject of the sentence. In practice, **watashi wa** can be discarded if it is clear that you are talking about yourself, and **ano eiga o mimashta** is thus sufficient. **ano eiga:** that movie (see above for 'that'), followed by **o** to show that the movie is the object of the verb.

mimashta: the past form of **miru**, to see.

Tanaka-san wa imass ka.
Is Mr Tanaka here/there? (Mr Tanaka – is – (question))

Tanaka-san is Mr (or Mrs, or Ms) Tanaka, followed by wa to indicate the subject of the sentence.

imass: present form of the verb iru, to be present.

Iru is used for people and animals; aru is used for objects.

Hon ga arimass there is a book
shonen ga imass there is a boy

ka: simply added to an otherwise normal sentence to turn it into a question, together with a suitable tone of voice. Question marks are not normally used in written Japanese.

Asking someone to do something

To ask or tell someone to do something, you must first make the -te form of the verb. For -ru and -su verbs, this is made by adding -te to the stem:

hanasu (to speak)   hanashite (pronounced hanashte)
miru (to see)   mite

For -ku verbs, add -ite to the stem:
kaku (to write)   kaite
aruku (to walk)   aruite

For -mu and -bu verbs, add -nde:
nomu (to drink)   nonde

yomu (to read)	yonde
yobu (to call)	yonde
erabu (to choose)	erande

For –tsu and –u verbs add –tte:

motsu (to carry)	motte
katsu (to win)	katte
kau (to buy)	katte
iu (to say)	itte

Add the word kudasai to the –te form to make it a request.

yamete kudasai Please stop (yameru, to stop or desist)
tasukete kudasai Help! (tasukeru, to help). Pronounced taskete.
kore o mite kudasai Please look at this (miru, to see or look at)

Note: to order someone to do something, just use the –te form on its own. This is abrupt, however, so only use it when you are issuing an order:

Yamete! Stop that!
Tomete! Stop the car! (From tomeru, to stop a vehicle)

The –te form of verbs is also used to make the continuous tense, by simply adding –imass or –imasen for the negative:

mite-imass (I am) watching mite-imasen (I am) not watching
yonde-imass (I am) reading yonde-imasen (I am) not reading

and the past by adding –imashta or imasen-deshta:

kīte-imashta (I was) listening (from kiku, to listen or hear)
kīte-imasen deshta (I was) not listening

Possessives

• •

The particle no is used to show possession:

Watashi no ashi My leg
Watashi no me My eye
Anata no kuruma Your car

It is also used to express the quality of belonging:

Nikkon no keizai Japan's economy (Nikkon, Japan – no – keizai, economy)

Natsu no atsusa The heat of summer (Summer natsu – no – heat atsusa, the heat that belongs to summer)

Adjectives

• •

Japanese adjectives fall into two groups: those that end in –i or ī, and those that have the word na after them. The former are more numerous.

atsui natsu (a) hot summer (natsu: summer)
omoi hon (a) heavy book (hon: book)
kirei na hito (an) attractive person (hito: person)
taisets na tegami (an) important letter (tegami: letter)

Some useful words

•••

In Japan, you will hear the word **ne** all the time. It is added to the end of sentences to show the speaker's agreement with what is being said, or (in a questioning tone) to show that agreement is being sought:

i dess ne! That's good, isn't it!
atsui dess ne! It's hot, isn't it!
karimass ne? I'm going to borrow this, OK? (**kariru**, to borrow)
Ne can also be used to attact a friend's attention, rather like 'hey'.

So: this translates as 'so' in the phrase 'I do it like so'. It means 'this way' or 'that way', and is used in some very common conversational phrases:

sō dess ka? Is that so? Literally, 'is that the way it is?' This is polite, and is used all the time. If you remove the questioning tone at the end, **sō dess ka** then means 'I see' or 'OK, so that's how it is').

sō dess ne! That's right, isn't it! (A very common phrase, mostly used simply to create a general air of agreement).

Dictionary

English – Japanese

A

a, an see grammar
abroad kaigai (ni)
abscess nōyō
accelerator aksēru
to accept: *do you accept credit cards?* kurejitto kādo demo ī dess ka?
accident (traffic, etc) jikō
accident and emergency department kyūkyū-byōtō
accommodation shukuhaku
account (bank) kōza
ache itami
my head aches atama ga itai dess
to act (do) suru
actor haiyū
actress joyū
adaptor (electrical) adaptā
address jūsho
what is the address? jūsho o oshiete kudasai
what is your address? go-jūsho o oshiete kudasai
this is my address watashi no jūsho dess
admission fee nyūjō-ryō
adult otona
advance: *in advance* maemotte
advance payment sakibarai
advertisement senden
to advise: *what do you advise?* dō sureba ī dess ka?
to afford: *I can't afford it* takasugimass
afternoon gogo
in the afternoon gogo ni

this afternoon kyō no gogo
again mata
(once more) mō ichi dō
age (person's) toshi; nenrei
(time) jidai
agenda (for meeting) kyōgi jikō
ago: *a week ago* isshūkan mae ni
to agree (support a proposal): *I agree* sansei shimass
do you agree? sansei shimass ka?
I don't agree sansei shimasen
to agree: *that's true, isn't it?* sō dess ne
let's do that sō shimashō
aid (charity) enjo
AIDS eizu
air kūki
air conditioning reibō
is there air conditioning? reibō ga arimass ka?
air hostess schuwadess
air pollution taiki osen
airline kōkū gaisha
airmail kōkūbin
airport kūkō
airport bus kūkō bass
alarm (in bank, shop) keihō
alarm call mōningu kōru
I'd like an alarm call at... ...ni mōningu kōru o onegai shimass
alarm clock mezamashi-dokei
alcohol arukōru
all subete (no)
allergic: *I'm allergic to shellfish* kai-rui no arerugī dess
allowed: *is it allowed?* ī dess ka?
alone hitori

I'm travelling alone hitori-tabi dess

always itsumo

a.m. (before noon) gozen

ambassador taishi

ambulance kyū-kyū-sha

please call an ambulance kyū-kyū-sha o yonde kudasai

America Amerika

American *adj* Amerika-no
(person) Amerika-jin

amount gaku; ryō

large amount kōgaku; tairyō

small amount shōgaku; shōryō

total amount sōgaku; sōryō

amusement park yūenchi

anaesthetic *n* masuizai

ancestor senzo

ancient kodai-no

and (furthermore) soshte
(noun and noun) to

angina anjaina; kyōshinshō

angry okotteiru

animal dōbuts

ankle ashi-kubi

anniversary kinenbi

wedding anniversary kekkon kinenbi

annoying: *it's very annoying* uttōshī; mukatsuku

annually maitoshi

another (a different kind) betsu no

I'd like another (a different kind) betsu no mono ga hoshī dess

another (one more) mō hitots

would you like another drink? mō ippai nomimass ka?

answer (written) henji
(spoken) kotae

there's no answer (on phone) daremo denwa ni demasen

answering machine russban denwa

antenna antena

antibiotic *n* kōsei busshits

antihistamine *n* kō-hisutamin-zai

antique *n* kottōhin

antiseptic *n* bōfuzai

anyone dare demo

anything nan demo

anywhere doko demo

apartment apāto

apologies: *my apologies!* (formal) owabi itashimass
(informal) gomen nasai

appendicitis mōchōen

appetite shokuyok

apple ringo

apple juice ringo jūs

application (job) mōshkomi

appointment yaksok

apricot anzu

April shigats

are: *are there any...?* ...ga arimass ka?

arm ude

armbands (for swimming) ude wa

to arrange: *can we arrange a meeting?* mīting o hiraitemo ī dess ka?

arrivals (airport) tōchak

to arrive tōchak suru

I will arrive at 8 pm gogo hachi-ji ni tōchak shimass

art geijuts; bijuts

art gallery bijuts-kan; āto gyararī

arthritis kansets-en

artichoke āchōku; kikuimo

artificial jinkō

artist geijuts-ka

as: *as soon as possible* dekiru dake hayaku

ashtray haizara
Asia Ajia
to ask tazuneru
asparagus asparagass; aspara
aspirin: *do you have any aspirin?*
  aspirin wa arimass ka?
assembly plant kumitate kō jō
assistant (shop) ten-in
asthma zensoku
I get asthma zensoku dess
at: *at home* uchi de
at 4 o'clock yoji ni
atmosphere (of place) funinki
attractive miryokuteki-na
aubergine nasu
audience (theatre etc) chōshū
August hachi-gatsu
aunt (own) oba
(somebody else's) oba-san
Australia ōstoraria
Australian *adj* ōstoraria-no
(person) ōstoraria-jin
author chosha
automatic (car) mishon-sha
autumn aki
available: *when will it be*
  available? itsu goro dekimass ka?
avalanche nadare
avenue tōri; namiki-michi
avocado abokado
to avoid sakeru
what food should I avoid? donna
  tabemono o sakeru-beki dess ka?
away: *I will be away in August*
  hachi-gats wa russ dess
awful hidoi

B

baby aka-chan
baby food rinyūshoku
baby milk bebi miruku

baby seat bebi shīto
babysitter bebi-shittā
baby wipes oshiri fuki
bachelor dokshin
I am a bachelor dokshin dess
back (of body) senaka
adv when will he be back? (kare wa)
  itsu modorimass ka?
I'd like to go back modoritai dess
bad (character, morally) warui
(food) kusatta
bag baggu; kaban
baggage nimots
baggage reclaim tenimots
  hikitori-jo
baker's pan-ya
ball bōru
banana banana
band (musical) bando; gakudan
bandage hōtai
bank ginkō
bar (to drink in) bā; izakaya
bar of chocolate choko bā
barbecue bābekyū
barber's toko-ya
bargain otoku
it's a bargain otoku dess
baseball yakyū
baseball game yakyū no shiai
basement chika
basket kago
basketball baskettobōru
bath furo
bathroom (toilet) otearai; toire
(bath) ofuro
bath towel basu taoru
bath tub ofuro
battery (for radio, etc) denchi
(for car) batterī
beach hama
bean (soya) mame

beancurd tōfu
beautiful utsukushī
how beautiful! nante utsukushī!
bed (western) beddo
(Japanese) ofuton
double bed daburu beddo
single bed shinguru beddo
bed and breakfast chōshoku-tski
  yado
bedding shingu; ofuton
bedroom shinshits
double (bedroom) daburu
single (bedroom) shinguru
bee sting: *I've been stung by a bee*
  hachi ni sasareta
beef gyūnik
beer bīru
bottled beer bin bīru
draught beer nama bīru
before …mae ni
before 4 o'clock yo-ji mae ni
before next week konshu chū ni
to begin hajimeru *v.t.*; hajimaru *v.i.*
to belong to: *it/they belong(s) to
  me* watashi no mono dess
does this belong to you? anata no
  mono dess ka?
belt beruto
beside: *can I sit beside you?* tonari
  ni suwatte ī dess ka?
best: *I like this best* kore ga
  ichiban ski dess
bicycle jitensha
big ōkī
bigger: *have you anything bigger?*
  motto ōkī mono wa arimass ka?
bike jitensha
mountain bike maunten baik
bill o-kanjō
can I have the bill, please? o-kanjō
  onegai shimass

binoculars bōenkyō
bird tori
birthday tanjōbi
happy birthday! tanjōbi o
birthday present tanjōbi
biscuits bisketto; kukkī
bit: *just a bit* hon no skos
to bite kamu
bitter (taste) nigai
it's too bitter for me nigasugimass
black *n* kuro
adj kuroi
blanket mōfu
bleach hyōhakuzai
to bleed: *it won't stop bleeding* chi
  ga tomaranai
blind *adj* me no mienai
(for window) braindo
blocked tsumatta
my nose is blocked (watashi no)
  hana ga tsumatte imass
the sink is blocked nagashi ga
  tsumatte imass
blood chi; ketsueki
blood group: *my blood group is…*
  (watashi no) ketsueki gata wa …
  dess
blood pressure: *I have high blood
  pressure* watashi wa kō ketsu-atsu
  dess
blue *n* ao
adj aoi
to board (plane, train) noru
boarding pass tōjō ken
boat bōto
(ship) fune
boiled rice gohan
bone hone
bonito katsuo
book (reading) hon
to book yoyak suru

...ke to book a flight to... ...yuki
...no bin o yoyak shtai dess
I'd like to book a table tēburu o
yoyak shtai dess
booking yoyak
booking office kipp uriba
booster seat būsta shīto
boots būtsu
(rubber) nagagutsu
to be born: *I was born in Scotland*
Skottorando de umaremashta
to borrow: *can I borrow...?*
...o karite ī dess ka?
botanical gardens shokubutsu-en
both ryōhō no
both A and B A to B no ryōhō
bottle bin; botoru
bottle opener sen-nuki
bowl bōru; wan
box hako
boy shōnen
boyfriend bōifrendo; kareshi
bra brajā
bracelet bresretto; udewa
brake fluid burēki eki
brake pads burēki ban
brakes burēki
please check the brakes burēki
o chekku shte kudasai
the brakes don't work burēki
ga kikimasen
branch (bank) shiten
(company) shisha
(of tree) eda
brandy burandē
bread pan
sliced bread suraisu breddo; kitta
pan
white bread shoku-pan
wholemeal bread komugi haiga
iri pan

to break kowasu
we've broken down koshō
shimashta
breakfast chōshoku; asa-gohan
breast (chicken) mune-niku
to breathe: *I can't breathe* iki
ga dekimasen
bride oyome; shinpu
bridegroom grūm; shinrō
bridge (game) brijji
(river, road, etc) hashi
briefcase kaban
to bring (thing) motte kuru
(person) tsurete kuru
please bring it to my room (watashi
no) heya ni motte-kite kudasai
would you like me to bring anything?
nani ka motte ikimashō ka?
Britain Igiriss; Eikoku
British adj Eikoku-no
(person) Eikoku-jin
brochure panfretto
do you have any brochures?
panfretto wa arimass ka?
broken: *this is broken* kore wa
kowarete imass
brothers kyōdai
older brother (own) ani
(somebody else's) o-nī-san
younger brother (own) otōto
(somebody else's) otōto-san
brown n cha-iro
adj cha-iro-no
Buddha hotoke
Buddhism bukkyō
Buddhist temple (o-)tera
building tatemono; biru
bulb (light) denkyū
bullet train Shinkansen
bureau de change ryōgae-sho
burn: *it's burnt* (food) kogete imass

bus bass
business (commerce) eigyō
(manufacturing) sangyō
(job) shigoto
business card meishi
business trip shu'chō
bus station bass ha'chakujo
bus stop bass tei
bus tour: *is there a bus tour?* bass tsuā wa arimass ka?
busy isogashī
are you busy? isogashī dess ka
the line's busy (phone) hanashi chū dess
butcher's nikuya
butter batā
button botan
to buy kau
where can I buy...? doko de … o kaemass ka?
by: *by bus* bass de
by car kuruma de
by plane hikōki de
by taxi takshī de
by train densha de

C

cab (taxi) takshī
cabaret kyabarē
cabbage kyabets
cabin (on ship) kyabin
cable car kēburukā; rōpuei
caddy (golf) kyadī
café kissaten
cake (western style) kēki
cake shop kēkiya
calculator keisanki
to call (phone) …ni denwa o kakeru
call (phone call) denwa
long-distance call chō kyori denwa
calm (person) ochitsuita

(weather) odayaka na tenki
camcorder bideo kamera; kamkōdā
camera kamera
camera bag kamera bagu
camera shop kamera-ya
camping kyanpu
can we go camping? kyanpu dekimass ka?
can *n* kan
can: *can I...?* …dekimass ka?
(may): *may I...?* …shtemo ī dess ka?
Canada Kanada
Canadian *adj* Kanada-no
(person) Kanada-jin
to cancel: *I'd like to cancel my booking* yoyaku o torikeshtai dess
cancellation (of flight) kekkō
(of train) unkyū
cancelled torikesareta
cancer gan
candle rōsok
canned kanzume
can opener kankiri
capital (city) shuto
(money) shikin
captain (ship) senchō
(plane) kyaputen
car kuruma; jidō sha
car accessories kuruma yō hin
caravan kyaraban; kyanping kā
card (business) meishi
(playing) toranpu
(greetings) kādo
cardboard box danbōru-bako
cardphone kādo yō denwa
careful: *be careful!* ki o tskete!
I will be very careful yoku ki o tskemas
careless: *how careless of me!* nante fuchūi nan deshō!

car hire rentakā
car keys kuruma no kagi
carp koi
car park chūshajō
carpet jūtan; kāpetto
carriage (train) kyakusha
carrier bag kaimonobukuro
carrot ninjin
to carry hakobu
carsick: I get carsick kuruma ni
  yoimass
carwash sensha
case (suitcase) sūtskēsu
cash n genkin
we only take cash genkin barai
  nomi dess
cash desk (o-)kaikei
cash machine ATM
can I use this cash machine? kono
  ATM o tsukattemo ī dess ka?
casino kajino
cassette kasetto
cassette player kasetto pureiyā
castle shiro
cat neko
to catch (hold of) tsukamu
to catch a cold kaze o hiku
cathedral dai-seidō
catholic katorikk kyōto
cauliflower karifurawā
cave dō kutsu
CD shīdī
CD player shīdī puraier
CD-Rom shīdī-rom
CD writer shīdī raitā
celery serori
cellphone keitai denwa
cemetery bochi
centigrade sesshi
centimetre senchimētoru; senchi
central heating danbō

centre chūshin; chūō
century seiki
21st century niju-isseiki
ceramics tōki
cereal (breakfast) shiriāru
certain: are you certain? hontō
  dess ka?
certainly (truth) tashika-ni
certainly! (I will do that) yorokonde!
certificate shōmeishō
chain (jewellery) kusari
chainstore chēn-ten
chair isu
chambermaid jochū
champagne shanpen
chalet bessō
change (money) kozeni
do you have any change? kozeni
  wa arimass ka?
to change: where can I change
  some money? doko de ryōgae (ga)
  dekimass ka?
do I need to change trains? densha
  o norikaeru hitsuyō ga arimass ka?
changing room kōi-shits
charge (fee) tesū-ryō
is there any charge? tesū-ryō wa
  kakarimass ka?
free of charge muryō
cheaper: do you have anything
  cheaper? motto yasui mono wa
  arimass ka?
to check chekk suru;
(investigate) shiraberu;
(car etc.) tenken suru
can you check this for me? kore o
  chekk shte kudasai
to check in: where do I check in?
  doko de chekk-in shimass ka?
check-in desk (hotel) furonto
to check out: when should I check

out by? chekk-auto wa nan-ji made dess ka?

cheers! kanpai!

cheese chīzu

chef shefu

chemist (scientist) kagaku-sha

chemist's (shop) kusuriya; yakkyok

cherry sakuranbo

cherry blossom sakura

chest (of body) mune

chestnuts kuri

chewing gum gamu

chicken (bird) niwatori

(meat) toriniku

(grilled) yaki-tori

chickenpox mizubōsō

children kodomotachi

do you have any children? o-kosan wa imass ka?

I don't have any children kodomo wa imasen

child seat chairudo shīto

chilli tōgarashi

china *n* setomono

China Chūgoku

Chinese *adj* Chūgoku-no

(person) Chūgoku-jin

(language) Chūgoku-go

chips (french fries) poteto-furai

(crisps) chipps

chocolate(s) chokorēto

to choose: *I don't know what to choose* dore ni sureba yoi no ka wakarimasen

you choose for me kawari ni erande kudasai

chopsticks (o-)hashi

Christian name senrei-mei

Christmas kurissmasu

Christmas Eve kurissmasu-ību

church kyōkai

is there a Protestant/Catholic church? purotesutanto/katorikk kyōkai wa arimass ka?

cigar hamaki

cigarette tabako

cigarette lighter raitā

do you have a light? hi wa arimass ka?

cinema (place) eigakan

city machi; tokai

city centre machi no chūshin

how do I get to the city centre? machi no chūshin ewa dō ikeba ī dess ka?

claim *n* yōkyū

to claim for yōkyū suru

class (in school) kumi; kurasu

business class bijiness kurass

economy class ekonomī kurass

first class fāsto kurass

second class sekando kurass

classical music kurashikku ongaku

clean *adj* kirei-na

to clean (house) sōji suru

can you clean this for me? kore o kirei ni dekimass ka?

it is not clean kirei de wa arimasen

cleaner (person) seisō gyōsha

clerk ten-in

clever kashikoi

climate kikō; fūdo

climbing (mountains) yama nobori; tozan

climbing boots tozan gutsu

cling film saran rapp

clinic kurinikku; shinryōjo

cloakroom kurōku; tenimots azukari-sho

where's the cloakroom? kurōku wa doko dess ka?

clock tokei

to close: *when do you close?* itsu

shimarimass ka?
close by chikaku
closed (shops) heiten
cloth nuno
clothes fuku
cloudy kumotte-iru
club kurabu
are you a member of a club? kurabu no kai-in dess ka?
clutch (car) kuratchi
coach (bus) bass
(of train) kyakusha
coach station bass noriba
coal sekitan
coast kaigan
coat kōto; uwagi
coat hanger hangā
I need more coat hangers motto hangā ga irimass
Coca Cola® kokakōra; kōk
cockroach gokiburi
coffee kōhī
black coffee burakku kōhī
cappuccino kapuchīno
decaffeinated coffee dekaf
white coffee miruku kōhī
coffee shop kissaten
cognac konyakk
coin koin; –dama
ten-yen coin ju-en-dama
cold: *it's cold* (room) samui dess
I have a cold kaze o hīte imass
I'm cold watashi wa samui dess
it's cold (food) samete-imass
colleague dōryō
to collect: *can you collect my luggage?* (watashi no) nimots o tori ni kimass ka?
when will it be collected? itsu tori ni kimass ka?
collect call korekuto kōru

college (university) daigaku
(junior college) tandai
colour iro
colourfast: *is it colourfast?* iro ga kawarimasen ka?
comb kushi
to come kuru
when can you come? itsu koraremass ka?
come in! dōzo!
comedy komedī
comfortable: *this is very comfortable* totemo kimochi ga ī dess
comics (publications) manga
commercial (on TV) komāsharu; shī em
common (usual) futsū-no; ippan
communism kyōsan shugi
compact disc konpakuto disuku; shīdī
company (firm) kaisha
company director (CEO) shachō
(chairman) jōmu
compartment (train) koshits
competition (business) kyōsō
(sports) taikai
competitive price kyōsō-kakaku
complaint: *I have a complaint* kujō ga arimass
to complete kansei suru
complicated: *it's very complicated* taihen fukuzats dess
composer sakkyoku-ka
compulsory: *is it compulsory?* kyōsei dess ka?
computer konpyūta
computer game konpyūta gemu
computer programmer konpyūta puroguramā
concert konsāto

concert hall konsāto hōru

concussion noshintō; gekidō

conditioner (hair) rinsu

condom kondōmu

conductor (music) shikisha

conference kaigi

conference centre kaigi jō

to confirm: *do I need to confirm?* kakunin suru hitsuyō ga arimass ka?

I want to confirm my booking yoyaku no kakunin o onegai shimass

congratulations omedetō gozaimass

connection (train, plane) noritsugi

(electronic) setsuzoku

constipated: *I'm constipated* benpi dess

consul ryōji

(ambassador) taishi

consulate ryōjikan

(embassy) taishikan

where is the British consulate? Igiriss ryōjikan wa doko dess ka?

contact details renraku-saki

contact lens cleaner kontakuto (renzu) kurīnā

contact lenses kontakuto (renzu)

continent tairik

contraceptive *n* hinin-yaku; hinin-yōhin

controls (car) sōjūsōchi; kontorō ru

convenient benri na

is it convenient for you? (anata ni totte) tsugō ga ī dess ka?

it isn't convenient for me (watashi ni totte) tsugō ga yoku arimasen

cook *n* kokku

(Japanese restaurants) itamae

to cook ryōri o suru

how do you cook this? dōyatte kore o ryōri shimass ka?

cooker rēnji

copy *n* kopī

can I make a copy? kopī o tottemo ī dess ka?

cork koruku

(bottle) botoru no sen

corkscrew sen-nuki

corn (sweetcorn, maize) tōmorokoshi

corner kado

correct: *is it correct?* tadashī dess ka?

corridor rōka

cost *n* kosuto

to cost: *how much does it cost?* ikura kakarimass ka?

cotton wata

cotton wool kiwata

cough *n* seki

to count kazoeru

counter (in shop, etc) kauntā

country (not town) inaka

(state) kuni

couple (people) kappuru; futari

courgettes zukkīni

courier kūriā

I want to send this by courier kūria de okuritai dess

course (study) kōza

(meal) kō su menyū

of course mochiron

court (law) hōtei; saiban

(tennis) kōto

cousin itoko

crab kani

crafts kōgeihin

cramp keiren

crayfish zarigani

cream kurīmu

creche hoikuen

credit shinyo
credit card (krejitto) kādo
cricket (game) kuriketto
crisps poteto chipps
cross n jūji
crossing (ferry): *when is the next crossing?* tsugi no ferī wa itsu dess ka?
crossroads jūjiro; kōsaten
crowd hitogomi
crown (on tooth) kuraun; shikan
cruise n funatabi; kurūz
to cry (weep) naku
cucumber kyūri
cup kappu
cupboard todana; mono-iri
cure (to heal) naosu
(remedy) **chiryōhō**
current (electricity) denryū
curtains kāten
cushion kusshon
(on tatami) zabuton
customs zeikan
customs declaration zeikan shinkoku
cut n kirikizu
to cut kiru
cute kawairashī; kawaī
cutlery hamono-rui
cybercafé intānet kafe
cycling saikuringu

D

daily (each day) mainichi-no
damage n higai
(scratches, dents) kizu
dance n odori
to dance dansu o suru; odoru
dangerous abunai; kiken
dark (colour) kurai
(deep) koi

date (day of month) hizuke
(formal appointment) hidori; yakusok
date of birth seinen-gappi
daughter (own) musume
(somebody else's) musume-san; o-jō-san
day hi; nichi
per day ichi nichi de
every day mai nichi
deaf nanchō
dear (expensive) kōka-na; takai
decaffeinated kafein nuki-no
December jū-ni-gats
deep fukai
degree (temperature) do
(university) gakui
delay: *how long is the delay?* donokurai okuremass ka?
to be delayed (plane, train, etc) okureru
dentist ha-isha
dentures ireba
deodorant bōshūzai; deodoranto
department store depāto; hyakkaten
departure shuppats
departure lounge shuppats raunji
deposit (to pay) hoshōkin
dessert dezāto
destination mokuteki-chi
detergent senzai
diabetes tōnyōbyō
to dial daiyaru suru
dialling code kyokuban
(country code) kuni-bangō
diarrhoea geri
diary nikki
dictionary jisho
diet daietto; shokuji ryōhō
different chigau
(things) betsu no

digital camera dejitaru kamera;
  dejikam
digital radio dejitaru rajio
dining room shokudō; dainingu
  rūmu
dinner yūshoku; bangohan
direct (train, etc) chokutsū
direction hōkō
directory jūsho-shimei-roku
dirty kitanai
disabled (person) shōgaisha
disco disuko
discount waribiki
dish (crockery) o-sara
(cookery) ryōri
disinfectant shōdoku-yaku
disk disuku
disposable tsukaisute-no
district chihō
divorce n rikon
divorced rikonshta
dizzy: to feel dizzy memai ga suru
to do suru (see grammar)
doctor isha; dokutā
document bunsho
dog inu
doll ningyō
dollar doru
door to; doā
double nijū-no
(quantity) nibai-no
double bed daburu beddo
double room daburu rūmu;
  futari beya
download daunrōdo suru
draught (air) sukima-kaze
(draught beer) nama bīru
to draw (picture) e o kaku
dress n doress; yōfuku
  v kigaeru
dressing (medical) hōtai

(salad) doreshingu
drink nomimono
to drink nomu
to drive unten suru
driver (of car) untenshu
driving licence unten-menkyoshō
drug (medical) kusuri; yakuhin
to dry (clothes, etc) kawakasu
dry-cleaner's dorai-kurīningu-ya
duck n ahiru
duty-free menzei-no
duvet kakebuton
DVD DVD
DVD drive DVD doraibu
DVD writer DVD raitā

E

each sorezore-no; kaku
each Wednesday maishū no
  suiyōbi
ear mimi
earache chūjien
early hayaku
earplugs mimi sen
earrings īyaringu
earthquake jishin
east higashi
Easter īsutā
to eat taberu
I don't eat eggs watashi wa tamago
  o tabemasen
I don't eat fish watashi wa sakana
  o tabemasen
I don't eat meat watashi wa nikk
  o tabemasen
edible shokuyō-no
eel (marine) unagi
(freshwater) anago
egg tamago
fried egg medama-yaki
hard-boiled egg kata yude tamago

...gs iri tamago;
...
...su
...gomu
...enkiya
...enki; denryoku
electric razor denki-kamisori
elevator erebētā
e-mail denshi mēru; ī mēru
this is my e-mail address watāshi
 no mēru adoress dess
to send an e-mail ī meru o okuru
embassy taishikan
emergency kinkyū
emergency exit hijōguchi
emperor tennō
empty kara
engaged (couple) kon-yaku shte-iru
(phone) hanashi-chū
(toilet) shiyō-chū

England Igiriss; Eikok
English *adj* Igiriss-no
(person) Igiriss-jin
(language) Eigo
enough: *that's enough* (food etc)
 mō kekkō dess
that's enough! (stop!) yamenasai!
enquiry desk uketsuke
to enter (a place) hairu
entrance iriguchi
entrance fee nyūjō-ryō
envelope fūtō
epileptic tenkan-no
epileptic fit tenkan sei keiren
equipment setsubi
escalator esukarētā
estate car see station wagon
euro yūro
Europe yōroppa
evening yoru; ban
in the evening yoru ni

evening meal yūshoku
example: *for example* tatoeba
excellent subarashī
excess baggage chōka nimots
exchange rate kawase rēto
excursion ensok
excuse me! (hailing; warning)
 sumimasen!
(apologising) shitsurei-shimashta
exhaust pipe haikikan
exhibition tenjikai
exit deguchi
expensive takai
exports yushutsu-hin
express train kyūkō
extension (electrical) enchō kōdo
(phone) naisen
extra (additional) yobun-no
eye me
eye drops megusuri

F

fabric kiji
factory kōjō
to faint kizetsu suru
fair (just) kōhei-na
(unfair) fukōhei-na
false teeth ireba
family kazoku
fan (hand-held) uchiwa; sensu
(electric) senpūki
fanbelt fanberuto
far tōi
fare (bus, etc) ryōkin
Far East Kyokutō
farm nōka
fast (speed) hayai
fat (person) futotta
father (own) chichi
(somebody else's) otō-san
faulty (machine, etc) kekkan no aru

fax fakks
fax number fakks bangō
my fax watashi no fakkus
to fax fakks o okuru
February ni-gats
fee ryōkin; daikin; -dai
female *adj* (human) onna-no
(animals) mesu
ferry ferī
festival matsuri
to fetch totte kuru
few: (two or three) ni san no
(too) few sukunai (sugiru)
fiancé(e) fianse; kon-yakusha
file (computer, document) fairu
to fill (up) mitasu; ippai ni suru
fill it up! ippai ni shte!
fill it up (gasoline) mantan kudasai
filling (tooth) tsumemono
film (for camera) firumu
(cinema) eiga
to find mitsukeru
I can't find... ...mitsukaremasen
fine (penalty) bakkin
finger yubi
fire: *house fire* kaji; kasai
camp fire takibi
fire alarm kasai-hōchi-ki; arāmu
fire brigade shōbōtai
fire escape hijōkaidan
fire extinguisher shōkakki
fireworks hanabi
firm (company) kaisha
(bed, etc.) katai
first saisho-no; hatsu
first aid okyū-teate
first aid kit kyūkyūbako
first class fāsuto kurass
first floor (above ground floor) nikai
first name namae
(another person's) onamae

fish *n* sakana
fishing (rod and line) tsuri
(commercial) gyogyō
to fit: *it doesn't fit* aimasen
fitting room shichaku shits
to fix: *can you fix it?* naose mass ka?
flat (apartment) apāto
(battery) batterī ga agaru
flat tyre panku
flavour aji
floor (of building) -kai
first floor (ground floor) ikkai
second floor ni-kai
(of room) yuka
flower hana
flu infuruenza
fly (insect) hae
to fly tobu
food tabemono
food poisoning shokuchū-doku
foot ashi
football (soccer) sakkā
for (in exchange for) ...no kawari ni
foreign gaikoku-no
forest mori
fork (cutlery) fōku
fortnight nishūkan
fountain funsui
four-wheel drive vehicle yonkusha
foyer robī
fracture (of bone) kossets
fragrance kaori
frame (picture) gaku
free (not occupied) aiteiru
(costing nothing) muryō-no
(not constrained) jiyū (na)
fresh (food) shinsen
Friday kin-yōbi
fridge reizōko

fried food agemono
friend tomodachi
fruit kudamono
fruit juice furūts jūs
fuel nenryō
fuel gauge nenryō kei
full (glass, stomach) ippai
(gasoline) mantan
I'm full onaka ga ippai dess
full board sanshok-tsuki no
  shukuhak
funfair yūenchi
funny (amusing) omoshiroi
(strange) okashī; kawatta
fuse hyūzu
fuse box hyūzu bokksu

G

gallery gyararī; garō
game (computer) gēmu
(baseball, soccer etc.) shiai
garage garēji
garden niwa
garlic nin-niku
gastritis ichōen; i-en
gate mon
(airport) gēto
gay (bright) hanayaka-na
(homosexual) gei
gears gīya
(cogs) haguruma
generous kandai-na
gentleman shinshi
gents (toilet) (dansei-yō) toire
genuine (things) honmono
(character) majime
to get (obtain) eru
(to fetch thing) motte kuru
(to fetch person, animal) tsurete kuru
to get in (car) noru
to get off (bus, etc) oriru

gift okurimono
gift shop gifuto shoppu;
  omiyage-ten
gigabyte gigabaito
gigahertz gigahātz
ginger shōga
girl shōjo
(polite) ojō-san
girlfriend kanojo; gārufurendo
to give ageru
to give back kaesu; modosu
glass guras
glasses (spectacles) megane
gloves tebukuro
glue nori
to go iku
to go back modoru
to go in hairu
gold kin
golf goruf
golf ball goruf bōru
golf club goruf kurab
golf course goruf kōs
good yoi; ī
good afternoon kon-nichi wa
goodbye sayonara
good evening konban wa
good morning ohayō gozaimass
good night oyasumi nasai
to go out dekakeru
granddaughter magomusume
grandfather (own) sofu
(somebody else's) ojī-san
grandmother (own) sobo
(somebody else's) obā-san
grandson magomusuko
grapefruit gurēpufurūtsu
grapes budō
great (large) ōkī
(person) erai
(experience) saikō

green *n* midori
  adj midori-no
greengrocer yaoya
grey *n* hai-iro; gurei
  adj hai-iro-no; gurei-no
grilled yaita; yaki-
grocer's shokuryōhin-ten
ground floor ikkai
group (people) gurūpu; dantai
guarantee *n* hoshō
guarantor hoshōnin
guard (on train) shashō; kakari'in
guest (to house) okyakusama
guest house gesuto hausu
guide *n* gaido; an-nai
to guide gaido o suru; an-nai
  o suru
guidebook gaidobukk
guided tour tsuā

H

hair kami; kami-noke
hairbrush heāburashi
haircut sanpats; katto
hairdresser's (for men) tokoya
  (for women) biyōin; saron
hair dryer heādoraiyā
hair gel heā no jeru
hairspray heāsuprē
half (of whole) hanbun
  (bottle) shobin
half-price hangaku-no
hall (for concerts, etc) hōru; kan
ham hamu
handbag (hando)baggu; kaban
hand brake saido burēki
handicapped shintaishōgai no aru
  (person) shogaisha
handkerchief hankachi
handle handoru; tesuri
hand luggage tenimots

hand-made tezukuri-no
to happen okoru
  (take place) okonau
what happened? dō shimashta ka?
hard (firm) katai
  (difficult) muzukashī
hard drive hādo doraibu
hat bōshi
hay fever kafunshō
head atama
headache zutsū
headlights hedoraito
head office honsha
headphones heddohōn
hearing aid hochōki
heart (emotional) kokoro
  (organ) shinzō
heart attack shinzōmahi
to heat up (food) atatameru
heater hītā
heavy (weight) omoi
hello kon-nichi wa
  (on phone) moshi moshi
to help tetsudau
help! taskete!
it can't be helped shikata ga nai
herb hābu; yakusō
here koko (ni)
high takai
high blood pressure kōketsu-atsu
high chair bebī cheya
hill-walking haikingu
to hire kariru
can I hire...? ...o kariremass ka?
hobby shumi
hole ana
holiday (from work) kyūka
on holiday kyūka-chū
national holiday saijits
homesick (to be) hōmushikk ni naru
honey hachimits

honeymoon hanemūn; shinkon ryokō
horse uma
horseradish (Japanese) wasabi
hospital byōin
host (at dinner, etc) shujin
hostel yūshu hosteru
hot atsui
I'm hot atsui dess
it's hot here atsui dess
hotel hoteru
Japanese hotel (traditional) ryokan
(B&B) minshuku
hot-water bottle yutanpo
hour jikan
one hour ichi-jikan
two hours ni-jikan
house ie
housewife shufu
house wine haus wain
how: *how much/many?* dono kurai?
how are you? o-genki dess ka?
hungry: *I'm hungry* onaka ga suite imass
hurry: *I'm in a hurry* isoide imass
to hurt: *(my back) hurts* (senaka ga) itai dess
husband (own) shujin
(somebody else's) go-shujin

I

I watashi
(polite) watakushi
ice kōri; aisu
ice cream aisukurīmu
identity card mibunshōmeisho
ignition key kākī
ill: *...is ill* ...wa byōki dess
illegal fuhō-no; ihō-no
immediately sugu-ni

important taisets (na)
imports yunyū
indigestion shōka furyō
indoors okunai de
inflammation enshō
information jōhō
information office annai-sho
inhaler kokyūki
injection chūsha
to be injured kega o suru
inquiry desk annai sho
insect konchū; mushi
insect repellent mushi-yoke
inside ...no naka ni
inside the car kuruma no naka ni
instant coffee instanto kōhī
instructions (for use) toriatsukai setsumei
instructor shidōsha; sensei
insulin inshurin
insurance hoken
insurance certificate hokenshō
international kokusaiteki (na)
Internet intānetto; uebu
Internet café intānetto kafe
interpreter tsūyakusha
interval (theatre) kyūkei
to introduce (a person) shōkai suru
invitation shōtai
to invite shōtai suru
invoice okurijō; seikyūsho
Ireland Airurando
Irish *adj* Airurando-no
(person) Airurando-jin
iron (for clothes) airon
(metal) tets
ironmonger's kanamono-ya
island shima
itemized bill seikyū meisaisho

J

jack (for car) jakki
jacket jakketto
jam (food) jamu
jammed (with people) komiatta
(paper in copier) tsumatta
traffic jam kōtsu jūtai
January ichi-gats
Japan Nihon; Nippon
Japanese (language) Nihongo
adj Nihon-no
(person) Nihon-jin
jeweller's hōseki-ten
jewellery hōseki-rui
job shigoto
to jog jogingu o suru
journey ryokō; tabi
juice (fruit) jūsu
(of something) shiru; eki
July shichi-gats
jump leads būstā-kēburu
junction (roads) kōsaten
June roku-gats
just: *just two* futats dake
I've just arrived tsuita bakari dess

K

key (for lock) kagi
kilo kiro
kilometre kiromētā
kind *n* shurui
adj shinsets-na
king kokuō; kingu
kitchen daidokoro
knickers panchī
knife naifu
(Japanese) hōchō
to knock down (car) (kuruma ga)
haneru
knot (in cord) musubime
(bump) kobu

to know (facts) shiru
I don't know Tokyo watashi wa
Tokyo o shirimasen
Korea Kankoku

L

label raberu; fuda
lace rēsu
shoe lace kutsu-himo
ladies (toilet) fujin-yō toire
lager ragā bīru
lake mizu-umi
lamb (meat) ramu
(animal) kohitsuji
land *n* tochi
land line (phone) ippan denwa
lane (narrow road) komichi
(on motorway) shasen
language gengo; kotoba
large ōkī
late osoi
the train is late densha ga okurete
imass
launderette koin randorī
laundry service kurīningu-ya
lavatory senmenjo
lawyer bengoshi
leader (of group) rīdā
leaflet chirashi
leak *n* (of gas, liquid) more
to learn manabu
leather kawa
to leave shuppats suru; saru
(leave behind) oite iku
left: *on/to the left* hidari ni
left luggage (office) tenimots ichiji
azukari-sho
leg ashi
lemon remon
lens renzu
lesson ressun; jigyō

letter (mail) tegami
(alphabet) moji
letterbox yūbin-bako
lettuce retasu
library toshokan
licence menkyosho; raisensu
to lie down yoko ni naru; nekorobu
lifebelt kyūmeigu
life boat kyūmei-bōto
life guard raifugādo; kyūjo-in
life jacket raifu jakketo
lift (elevator) erebētā
v ageru
light: *do you have a light?* hi wa arimass ka?
light bulb denkyū
lighter raitā
lightning inazuma
to like: konomu; suki
I like coffee kōhī ga suki dess
I'd like... ...ga hoshī dess
like this kono yō ni; kō iu fū ni
lime raimu
line (railway) sen; rain
(drawn) rain
lip-reading shiwahō; dokushin-juts
lipsalve kuchibiru yō nankō
list hyō; risuto
to listen to... ...o kiku
litre rittoru
little: *a little* sukoshi
(small) chīsai
to live (in a place) sumu; kurasu
I live in London Rondon ni sunde imass
(to be alive) ikiru
(he) is alive (kare wa) ikitteimass
liver rebā
living room ima
lobster (Western) robstā
(Japanese) Ise-ebi

local (wine, speciality) jimoto-no
lock (on door, box) kagi; rokk
to lock kagi o kakeru
locker rokkā
long nagai
for a long time nagai aida
to look for sagasu
loose (not fastened) yurui
to lose: *I've lost...* ...o naku shimashta
lost (object) nakushta
lost-property office ishitsubuts toriatsukaijo
lot: *a lot* takusan
lotion rōshon
loud (person) koe no ōkī
(surroundings) yakamashī; sōzōshī
lounge (in hotel) raunji
love n ai
I love swimming suiei ga daiski dess
low-alcohol tei alkōru no
luggage tenimots
luggage allowance tenimots seigen
luggage rack (in car, train) amidana
luggage trolley nimots tororī; daisha
lunch hiru gohan; ranchi
luxury zeitaku

M

machine kikai
magazine zasshi
maid jochū; meido
(polite) jochū-san; meido-san
mail n yūbin
by mail yūbin de
e-mail mēru
mains (electric) honkan
to make tsukuru

make-up (o-)keshō
man (general) hito
(male) otoko
manager sekininsha; manējā
many takusan-no; ōku no
map chizu
marathon marason
March san-gats
market ichiba; māketto
marmalade māmarēdo
to get/be married kekkon suru
(they/we are) a married couple
 fūfu dess
martial arts budō
mask kamen; masku
mass (in church) misa
match (game) shiai
matches matchi
material (fabric) kiji
to matter: it doesn't matter
 kamaimasen
what's the matter? dō shimashta ka?
mattress mattoresu
May go-gats
meal shokuji
to mean: what does this mean?
 kore wa dō iu imi dess ka?
meat (o-)nik
mechanic kikaikō; mekkanik
medical insurance iryō-hoken
medicine (pills, etc.) kusuri
(science) igaku
medieval chūsei-no
to meet au
let's meet again mata aimashō
meeting mītingu; kaigi
megahertz megahātz
member (of club, etc) kai-in; menbā
menu menyū
message dengon; messeiji
metre mētā

microwave chin
to microwave chin suru
midday ohiru
at midday ohiru ni
middle-aged chūnen-no
midnight mayonaka
migraine henzutsū
mile mairu
milk miruku; gyūnyū
semi-skimmed teishibō gyūnyū
soya milk tōnyū
millimetre mirimētoru
million n hyaku-man
adj hyaku-man-no
mineral water mineraru uōtā
minibar mini bā
minute (unit of time) fun
one minute ippun
two minutes nifun
minute (very small) goku chīsai
mirror kagami
to miss (train, etc) norisokonau
missing (person) yukuefumei-no
mistake n machigai
misunderstanding: there must be
 a misunderstanding gokai ni
 chigai arimasen
mobile phone keitai denwa
mobile phone charger keitai
 judenki
modem mōdemu
monastery shūdōin
Monday getsu-yōbi
money (o-)kane
I have no money watashi wa okane
 ga arimasen
month tsuki
moon tsuki
more: more wine please motto
 wain o kudasai
no more thank you mo kekkō dess

morning asa
(a.m.) gozen
in the morning gozenchū ni
this morning kesa
mosquito ka
mother (own) haha
(somebody else's) okā-san
motor mōtā; hatsudōki
motorbike ōtobai; baik
motorboat mōtā bōto
motorway kōsoku dōro
mountain yama
mountain bike maunten baik
mountain rescue sangaku kyūjotai
mouse (animal) nezumi
(computer) mausu
mouth kuchi
Mr... ...-shi; ...-san
Mrs... ...-san; ...-fujin
Ms... ...-san
much: *there's too much* ōsugiru
mugged: *I've been mugged*
  tachidorobo saremashta
museum hakubutsu-kan
mushroom masshurūmu
(Japanese) kinoko-rui
(kinds include) shītake; matsutake
music ongaku
mussel murasaki igai; mūru-gai

N

nail (finger) tsume
(metal) kugi
name namae
what's your name? o-namae wa
  nan dess ka?
nappy omutsu
narrow semai
nationality kokseki
nausea hakike
near chikaku ni

near the bank ginkō no chikaku (ni)
necessary hitsuyō-na
(unnecessary) fuhitsuyō-na, yokei na
neck kubi
necklace nekkuress
to need: *I need...* ...ga irimass
needle hari
negative (photograph) nega
neighbour kinjo no hito
nephew oi
never *adv* kesshte ... masen
I never drink wine kesshte wain o
  nomimasen
new atarashī
news nyūsu; (o-)shirase
newspaper shinbun
New Year shin'nen
(New Year's holiday) o-shōgats
New Zealand Nyū jīrando
New Zealander (person) Nyū
  jīrando-jin
next: *next week* raishū
next year rainen
the next train tsugi no densha
night yoru
at night yoru (ni)
last night sakuya; yūbe
tomorrow night ashta no yoru
nightclub naito kurabu
nightdress nemaki
no īe
no thank you īe kekkō dess
noisy yakamashī; urusai
non-alcoholic arukōru nuki-no
non-smoking kinen
non-smoking compartment kinen
  sharyō
noodles (general) men-rui
(kinds include) udon; soba; ramen
noon ohiru
north kita

Northern Ireland Kita Airurando
note (banknote) shihei
(letter) tsūtats; memo
November jū-ichi-gats
now ima
nowadays konogoro
number (of) kazu
(written) sūji
number 1, 2 etc. ichiban, niban etc
  (see numbers)
numberplate (on car) nanbā pureito
nurse kangofu
nut (peanut, etc) nattsu
(for bolt) tome-neji

O

object (thing) mono
October jū-gats
octopus tako
of (possessive) ...no
edge of the table tēburu no hashi
Queen of England Igiriss no jō-ō
off (light) kieteiru
(food) kusatteiru
office ofisu; jimusho
often yoku
oil (cooking, lubrication) abura
(petroleum) sekiyū
oil filter oirufirutā
oil gauge oiru kei
ointment nankō
OK: *I'm OK, it's OK* kekkō dess;
  daijōbu dess
OK, let's do that ō-kei; sō
  shimashō
old (things) furui
(people) toshiyori
how old are you? nan sai dess ka?
olive orību
omelette omurets
on (light) tsuiteiru

on the table tēburu no ue ni
one see section on counting
one-way ticket katamichi kippu
onion tamanegi
to open (box, etc) akeru
(shop) kaiten suru
(open up) hiraku
the door is open dōa ga aitteimass
the shop is open eigyō chu dess
what time does it open? nanji ni
  akimass ka?
operation (medical) shujuts
opposite (hand, side) hantai-no
opposite (meaning) gyaku
optician megane-ya
orange *adj* orenji-iro-no
(fruit) orenji
orange juice orenji jūsu
order: *out of order* koshō-chū
out (light) kieteiru
(he's) out (kare wa) gaishuts-chū
  dess; dete-imass
outdoor (pool, etc) kogai-no
oven ōbun
overnight: *to spend one night*
  ippak suru
overnight train yakō densha
oysters kaki
ozone ozon

P

pacemaker pēsmēkā
Pacific Ocean taiheiyō
packet kozutsumi
painful itai
painkiller chintsūzai; itadome
painting e
oil painting abura-e
pair: *a pair of shoes* kutsu issok
palace kyūden
pants (trousers) zubon

(men's underwear) pantsu
(women's underwear) panchī
paper (drawing, wrapping) kami
(newspaper) shinbun
paper handkerchief tisshu
paper towels kami taoru; kitchen pepā
pardon? sumimasen
(I didn't hear/understand) mō ichido onegai shimass
parents ryōshin
your parents go-ryōshin
park (garden) kōen
parking lot chūsha-jo; pākingu
partner (wife) oku-san
(husband) danna
party (evening) pātī
(group) ikkō; ichidan
pass (permit) kyokashō
passenger jōkyaku
passport paspōto
passport control shutsunyūkoku kanrisho
path komichi
to pay harau
payment shiharai
payphone kōshū denwa
peach momo
peanut pīnatts
pear (Japanese) nashi
(western) yōnashi
pearl shinju
pedestrian *n* hokōsha
pedestrian crossing ōdanhodō
pen pen
pencil enpits
penicillin penishirin
penfriend penfurendo
pensioner nenkin-juryōsha
people (persons) hitobito
(folk, race) jinrui

people carrier wanbox-kā
pepper (spice) koshō
(vegetable) pīman
per: *per hour* ichijikan nitsuki
per person hitori nitsuki
per week isshukan nitsuki
percent pāsento
performance pafōmansu
perfume kōsui
period (menstruation) seiri; gekkei
(time) kikan
(historical) jidai
permit (authorisation) kyokashō
(drivers' license) menkyoshō
persimmon kaki
person hito
personal organizer denshi techō
personal stereo uōkman
petrol gasorīn
petrol station gasorīn stando
petrol tank (in car) gasorīn tank
pharmacy yakkyoku
phone *n* denwa
to phone denwa o kakeru
phone box denwa boks
phonecard terehon-kādo
phone number denwa-bangō
photocopy *n* kopī
to make a photocopy kopī o suru
photograph *n* shashin
shashin o toru
phrase book seiku jiten
picnic pikunik
picture (painting) e
(photo) shashin
pig buta
pill kusuri
contraceptive pill piru
pillow makura
PIN number anshō bangō
pineapple painappuru

plan (of a building) zumen
to plan kikaku suru
plane (aircraft) hikōki
plaster (sticking plaster) bando-eido
plastic bag pori-bukuro
platform (railway) hōmu
play (theatre) geki
please (permitting) dōzo
(requesting) kudasai; onegai shimass
plug (electrical) puragu; sashikomi
plug socket konsento
plum (Japanese, green) ume
(western, purple) puram
plumber haikankō; suidōya
p.m. (after noon) gogo
poisonous yūdoku-na
police keisats
policeman keisats kan
(patrolman) omawari-san
police station kōban
pool (swimming) pūru
pork buta-niku
porter (hotel) pōtā
portion (of food) ichinin-mae
postbox yūbin-bako
postcard e-hagaki; postokādo
post office yūbin-kyok
potato jagaimo
pottery tōki-rui; setomono
pound pondo
power (outlet) konsento
power cut teiden
prawn tenaga-ebi; kuruma-ebi
pregnant ninshin shte iru
prescription shohōsen
present n okurimono; prezento
v ageru; sashiageru
president (of a company) ...shachō
pretty kirei-na
price nedan
priest (Buddhist) sōryo

(Catholic) shimpu
(Protestant) bokushi
prime minister sōridaijin
prince ōji
(crown prince) kōtaishi
princess ōjo
printout purintauto
private kojin-no; puraibetto
prize shōhin
problem mondai
there's a problem mondai ga
 arimass
programme (TV, etc) bangumi
(computer) puroguram
promise: it's a promise yaksok dess
to pronounce: how is it
 pronounced? dō hatsuon shimass
 ka?
Protestant shinkyōto
prune purūn
public holiday saijits
public toilet koshū benjo
to pull hiku
puncture panku
puppet ayatsuri ningyō
pure (gold, silver, etc) junsui-na
purse saifu
push osu
pushchair buggi/bebīkā

Q

qualification shikaku
quality hinshits
queen jō-ō
question n shitsumon
queue retsu
to form a queue retsu o tsukuru
quickly hayaku
quiet (place) shizuka-na
(person) odayaka-na
quilt kiruto

R

rabies kyōkenbyō
race (sport) kyōsō; rēsu
(people) jinshu
radio rajio
radish (small, red) radish; hatsuka
  daikon
(Japanese) daikon
raft rāfuto
railway station eki
rain ame
it's raining ame ga futte imass
rare (unique) mare-na
(steak) rea; namayake
rash (skin) hasshin
rate (of exchange) rēto
raw nama
razor kamisori
razor blades kamisori no ha
ready junbi ga dekita
receipt ryōshusho; reshīto
reception (desk) uketsuke
receptionist uketsukegakari
to recharge (battery) saijūden suru
recipe reshipī; chōrihō
to recommend: *what do you
  recommend?* nani ga osusume
  dess ka?
record (music, etc) rekōdo
red *n* aka
adj akai
reduction (for student, etc) waribiki
refreshments keishoku
refund: *I'd like a refund* henkin
  shte kudasai
region chi'iki; chihō
to reimburse hensai suru
relative (family member) shinseki
relatively (comparitively) hikakuteki
reliable (person) shinrai dekiru
religion shūkyō

to remember omoidasu
to rent kariru
rent (for house, flat) yachin
to repair shūri suru; naosu
repeat: *would you repeat that,
  please?* mō ichidō itte kudasai
reservation yoyaku
reserved yoyaku-shta
reserved seat shitei-seki
resort (seaside) rizōto
rest (relaxation) kyūsoku
to rest kyūsoku suru
restaurant restoran
restaurant car shokudōsha
restroom toire
retired intai shta; taishoku shta
to return (to go back) kaeru; modoru
(to give back) kaesu
(to return a purchase) henpin suru
return ticket ofuku-ken
reverse-charge call (collect call)
  korekuto kōru
rheumatism ryūmachi
rice okome
(cooked) gohan
rich (food) nōkō-na
(person) yūfuku-na; okanemochi
riding (horse) jōba
to go horse riding jōba ni iku
right (correct) tadashī
on/to the right migi ni
(legal) kenri
(human right) jinken
ring (for finger) yubiwa
river kawa
road michi; dōro
road map dōro chizu
road sign dōro hyōshiki
to roast, bake or grill yaku
room (in house, hotel) heya
(space) basho

it takes up room basho o torimass
room service rūmu sābisu
rotten (meat, fruit) kusatta
roundabout (in road) rōtarī
roundabout route mawari-michi
route rūto
row (theatre, etc) retsu
royal kokuō-no; ōshitsu-no
rubbish gomi
(nonsense) tawagoto
rucksack ryukkusak
rush hour rasshu

S

safe *adj* anzen-na
safety belt anzenberuto;
 shītoberuto
safety pin anzen pin
sailing (sport) seiringu
salad sarada
salary sararī; kyūryō
sale (in shops) sēru; bāgen
sales tax shōhizei
salesman seirusuman
(in store) ten-in
salmon sake
salt shio
sandals sandaru
sandwich sandoitchi
sanitary towel seiriyō napukin
sardine iwashi
satellite TV eisei terebi
Saturday do-yōbi
sauce (Worcestershire) sōsu
(Soy) oshōyu
to save (life) sukuu
(money) takuwaeru; chokin suru
to say iu
scales (for weighing) hakari
scenery keshiki
school gakkō

(grad school) daigakuin
scissors hasami
Scotland Skottorando
Scottish *adj* Skottorando-no
screen gamen
screw *n* neji
screwdriver doraibā
scuba diving skyūba daibing
sculpture (object) chōkoku
sea umi
seafood shīfūdo; kaisan ryōri
sea sickness funayoi
seaside: *at the seaside* umibe de
season (of year) kisets
season ticket (transport) teiki-
 jōshaken
seat seki
seat belt shītoberuto
seaweed kaisō
(edible) nori
second *adj* dai ni-no
second class nikyū; nitō
secretary hisho
security guard kēibi'in
seashell kaigara
to see miru
self-catering jisui-no
self-service serufu sābisu
to sell uru
Sellotape® serotēpu; skochtēpu
to send okuru
to send someone off miokuru
senior citizen kōrēi-sha
September ku-gats
service charge sābisuryō
set menu teishoku
sex sekks
shampoo shanpū
to share buntan suru; wakeru
shares (stocks) kabu
to shave soru

shaving cream higesori kurīmu
sheet shītsu
shellfish kai-rui
ship fune
shirt shatsu
shock (electric) kanden
shock absorber shok abusōbā
shoe kutsu
shoe laces kutsu-himo
shoe polish kutsu-migaki
shop mise
shopping kaimono
to go shopping kaimono ni iku
shopping trolley shopping kāto
short cut chikamichi
shorts hanzubon
shoulder kata
show (at theatre, etc) shō
shower shawā
shrimps ko-ebi
shrine jinja
to shut shimeru
sick (ill) byōki-no
to be sick (vomit) haku
sightseeing kankō
signal: *there's no signal* hasshin
  ga arimasen
signature sain
silk kinu
silver *n* gin
  adj gin-no
single (person) dokshin
(bed, room) hitori yō no
(ticket) katamichi
sink (bathroom etc) nagashi;
  senmendai
sister (own, younger) imōto
(older) ane
(somebody else's, younger) imōto-san
(older) onēsan
size ōkisa

(clothes) saizu
skateboard sukētobōdo
skating (ice) aisu sukēto
(roller) rōrā sukēto
to ski skī o suru
ski boots skīgutsu
ski lift skīrifuto
ski pass lifto ken
skirt sukāto
to sleep nemuru
lack of sleep nebusoku
sleeping bag nebukuro
sleeping mat surīpingu matto
sleeping pill suimin-yaku
slippers surippa
slow osoi
small chīsai
smell *n* nioi
to smell of... ...no nioi ga suru
to smoke tabako o suu
smoking: *no smoking* kin-en
smoking compartment kitsuensha
sms message keitai mēru
snack karui shokuji; keishok
snorkeling sumoguri; shunōrukeru
snow *n* yuki
it's snowing yuki ga futteimass
snowboard(ing) sunōbōdo
soap sekken
soap powder kona sekken; senzai
sober (not drunk) shirafu-no
sock sokkus; kutsushta
socket (electrical) konsento
soda water tansan sui
soft drink softo dorinku
something nani ka
shall we eat something? nani ka
  tabemashō ka?
sometimes tokidoki
son (own) musuko
(somebody else's) musuko-san

song uta
soon sugu; mamonaku
sore: *sore head* zutsū
sore throat nodo no itami
sorry: *I'm sorry* sumimasen
soup sūpu
south minami
South Africa Minami Afrika
South African (person) Minami
 Afrika-jin
souvenir omiyage; kinenhin
soy sauce shōyu
spa onsen
spanner renchi
spare parts pāts; buhin
spare tyre supeā taiya
spark plug supāk puragu
to speak: *do you speak English?*
 Eigo o hanasemass ka?
speciality (academic) senmon
(of restaurant, region etc.) meibuts
speed limit seigen sokudo
to spell: *how is it spelt?* tsuzuri
 o oshiete kudasai
to spend (money) (okane o) tsukau
spicy karai
spirits (alcohol) jōryūshu
spoon supūn
sport supōts
sprain (ankle, etc) nenza
spring (season) haru
(hot) onsen
(mechanical) bane
squash (game, drink) sukassh
squid ika
stadium sutajiam; kyōgijō
stamps (for letters) kitte
star (in sky) hoshi
(film) sutā
station eki
station wagon wagon-sha

stationer's bunbōgu-ya
statue zō
steak stēki
steep kyū-na; kewashī
stereo stereo
sterling igiriss pondo
sticking plaster bansōkō;
 bando eido
sting *n* sashi-kizu
stomach onaka
(medical) ibukuro
stomachache fukutsū
storm arashi
storey kai
second storey ni-kai
story hanashi
straight on massugu
strange (odd) hen-na
strawberry sutoroberī; ichigo
street tōri
street map (residential) jūtaku chizu
(road) dōro chizu
string (for wrapping) himo
stroll: *to go for a stroll* sanpo suru
strong (person) tsuyoi
(material) jōbu na
stuck (jammed) tsumatte iru
student gakusei
stung: *I've been stung*
 sasaremashta
suburbs kōgai
subway (metro) chikatets
suddenly totsuzen
sugar satō
sugar-free mutō
suit (man's) shinshi yō sūts
(woman's) fujin yō sūts
suitcase sūtsukēs
summer natsu
sun taiyō
to sunbathe nikkōyoku o suru

sunburn hiyake
Sunday nichi-yōbi
sunglasses sangurass
sunrise hi no de
sunscreen hiyake-dome
sunset yūyake
sunshade parasoru
sunstroke nisshabyō
suntan lotion hiyake rōshon
supermarket sūpāmāketto; sūpā
supper (dinner) yūshoku
supplement *n* furoku
surgery (of doctor) shinsatsu-shits
(operation) shujutsu
surname myōji
suspension (of car) saspen
sweet (not savoury) amai
sweetener kanmiryō
sweets (boiled) ame
(general) okashi
to swim oyogu
swimming pool suimingu pūru
swimsuit mizugi
to switch off suitchi o kiru
to switch on suitchi o ireru
synagogue yudaya-kyōkaidō

T

table tēburu; tsukue
to take: how long does it take?
 dono kurai kakarimass ka?
take me home ie made okutte
 kudasai
to talk hanasu
tampon tanpon
tangerines mikan
tap jaguchi
tape (sticky) nenchak tēpu
(audio) kasetto tēpu
to taste (of something) ajiwau
to taste (something) tabete miru

tax zeikin
tax-free menzei-no
taxi takshī
taxi driver takshī no untenshu
taxi rank takshī noriba
tea (green) o-cha
(black) kōcha
teacher sensei
teenager chīnējā
teeth ha
telephone *n* denwa
telephone box denwa boks;
 kōshū denwa
to make a telephone call denwa
 o suru
telephone directory denwa chō
telephone number denwa bangō
television terebi
to tell iu; tsutaeru
(to announce or report) noberu
(to distinguish) wakaru
temperature (air) kion
(water) suion
to have a temperature netsu ga aru
temple (o)tera
tennis tenis
tennis court tenis kōto
tennis racket tenis raketto
tent tento
terminal (airport) tāminaru
text message keitai mēru
thank you arigatō
thank you very much (dōmo)
 arigatō gozaimass
that see grammar
the see grammar
theatre gekijō
thermometer ondokei
thick (paper, board) atsui
(rope, cord) futoi
(sauce) koi

thief dorobō
thin (paper, sauce) usui
(rope, cord) hosoi
thing mono
my things watashi no mono
thirsty: *I'm thirsty* nodo ga kawaite
imass
this see grammar
thread ito
throat nodo
thunder kaminari
thunderstorm raiu
Thursday moku-yōbi
ticket kippu; chiketto
ticket adjustment machine
norikoshi seisanki
ticket adjustment window
norikoshi seisan madoguchi
ticket office kippu uriba
ticket vending machine kippu
hanbai-ki
tight kitsui
tights taits
time jikan
this time konkai
what time is it? nan-ji dess ka?
timetable sukejūru
(train, etc) jikoku-hyō
tinned kanzume
tinfoil arumi hōiru
tin-opener kankiri
tired: *I'm tired* (watashi wa)
tsukarete imass
tissue tisshu
toast tōsto
tobacconist's tabako-ya
today kyō
toilet toire; benjo
(polite) o-tearai
toilet paper toiretto pēpā
toiletries keshōhin

toll tsūkōryō
tomato tomato
tomorrow asu; ashta
tomorrow morning ashta no asa
tomorrow afternoon ashta no gogo
tomorrow evening ashta no yugata
tomorrow night ashta no yoru
tonic water tonik uōtā
tonight kon ya
tooth ha
toothache haita
toothbrush haburashi
toothpaste hamigaki
torch kaichū dentō
tough (meat) katai
(person) tafu
tour (sightseeing) tsuā
tourist kankō-kyaku
tourist office kankō-annai-sho
towel taoru
town machi
town centre machi no chūshin
town plan toshi-keikaku
tow rope kenin rōpu
toy omocha
tracksuit torēningu uea
tradition dentō
traffic kōtsū
traffic jam kōtsū jūtai
traffic lights shingō
train densha
translation hon'yaku
translator tsūyaku
to travel ryokō o suru
travel agent ryokō dairiten
traveller's cheque toraberāzu
chek
tray (o-)bon
tree ki
trip (travel) ryokō; tabi
(trip and fall) kokeru

trousers zubon
trout masu
true (real) hontō-no
trunk (luggage) toranku
(body) dōtai
to try: *can I try it on?* shichaku dekimasu ka?
Tuesday ka-yōbi
tuna tsuna; maguro
to turn off (light, etc) kesu
to turn on (light, etc) tsukeru
tweezers pinsetto
twice nikai
twin-bedded room tsuinbeddo no heya
tyre taiya
tyre pressure taiya atsu

U

ulcer kaiyō
umbrella kasa
umpire shinpan
uncle (own) oji
(somebody else's) oji-san
underground (metro) chikatets
underpants (man's) shtagi
to understand: *I don't understand* wakarimasen
do you understand? wakarimass ka?
underwear shtagi
unemployed mushoku-no
United Kingdom Eikoku; Igiriss
United States (of America) (Amerika) Gasshūkoku; Beikoku
university daigaku
to unpack (case) ni o hodoku; ni o toku
unreserved seat jiyū-seki
urgent kinkyū-no
USB flash drive donguri; USB doraibu

USB port USB pōto
usually futsū ni; fudan ni

V

vacancy (in hotel) kūshits
vaccination yobō chūsha
valid (passport, etc) yūkō na
valuables kichōhin
van ban; wanbox kā
vase tsubo; kabin
veal (meat) ko-ushi no niku
vegetable yasai
vegetarian bejetarian
vehicle norimono
very taihen; totemo
video bideo
video camera bideo kamera
video cassette bideo kasetto
video game bideo gēmu
village mura
vinegar su
virus uiras
visa biza
to visit tazuneru
visitor kyaku
(tourist) kankōkyaku
vitamin bitamin
volt boruto
how many volts? nan boruto?
voltage den-atsu

W

wage chingin; kyūryo
waist koshi
to wait for... ...o matsu
waiter ueitā
waiting room machiai-shits
waitress uētoress
wake up okiru
Wales Uēruzu
walk: *to go for a walk* sanpo ni iku

wallet saifu
to want hoshigaru
wardrobe yōfuku-dansu
warm atatakai
(lukewarm) nurui
(to warm something up) atatameru
to wash arau
washing machine sentaku-ki
washing-up liquid ekitai senzai
washing powder kona sekken
wasp suzumebachi
watch (on wrist) udedokei
to watch TV terebi o miru
water mizu
cold water mizu
hot water oyu
waterfall taki
water heater yuwakashiki
watermelon suika
waterproof bōsui-no
water-skiing suijō-skī
way (manner) shikata
(route) hōkō
way in iriguchi
way out deguchi
we watashi-tachi
weak (physically) yowai
(tea, etc) usui
weather tenki
weather forecast tenkiyohō
website uebusaito
wedding kekkon shiki
Wednesday sui-yōbi
week shū
last week senshū
next week raishū
this week konshū
weekday heijits
weekend shūmats
weekly maishū-no
weight omosa

well: *well done* yoku dekimashta
I am well genki dess
Welsh (person) uēruzu-jin
west *n* nishi
adj nishi-no
(western world) seiyō
wet nureta
(soaking wet) bisho-bisho
what nani; nan
what is it? sore wa nan dess ka?
wheel (of car) sharin; hoīru
(steering wheel) handoru
wheelchair kuruma-iss
when? itsu?
where? doko?
which: *which is it?* dore dess ka?
whisky uiskī
white *n* shiro
adj shiroi
who dare
wholemeal bread komugi haiga
iri pan
whose: *whose is it?* dare no
dess ka?
why: *why is...?* naze...?
why did you...? doshte...?
wide hiroi
widow mibōjin
widower otoko-yamome
wife (own) tsuma; kanai
(somebody else's) okusan
WiFi waifai; musen
to win katsu
wind (air) kaze
window mado
windscreen fronto garasu
windscreen wipers waipā
windsurfing uindo sāfin
wine wain
house wine haus wain
red wine aka wain

white wine shiro wain
wine list wain risto
winter fuyu
wire (electric) kōdo
wireless (network) musen
(appliance) kōdoress
with (a person) ...to issho ni
woman onna
wonderful subarashī
wood ki
wood carving (object) kibori
wool ke; uru
word tango
to work (person) hataraku
(machine, car) ugoku
world sekai
worse sara ni hidoi
worth: *it's worth...* ...no kachi
  ga arimass
wrapping paper hōsō-shi
wrist tekubi
to write kaku
writer (author) chosha
writing paper binsen
wrong warui

X

x-ray x-sen

Y

yacht yotto
year: *for one year* ichi–nen–kan
one year old issai
five years old go–sai
last year kyonen
next year rainen
yearly maitoshi-no
yellow *n* ki-iro
adj ki-iro-no
yes hai; e
yes please hai onegai shimass
yesterday kinō
yet: *not yet* mada
youth hostel yūsu hosuteru

Z

zebra crossing ōdan hodō
zero zero; rei
zip chakku; fasunā
zip code yūbin bangō
zone zōn; chitai
zoo dōbutsu-en
zucchini zukkīni

Further titles in Collins' phrasebook range
Collins Gem Phrasebook

Also available as **Phrasebook CD Pack**

Other titles in the series

Afrikaans	Japanese	Russian
Arabic	Korean	Thai
Cantonese	Latin American	Turkish
Croatian	Spanish	Vietnamese
Czech	Mandarin	Xhosa
Dutch	Polish	Zulu
Italian	Portuguese	

Collins Phrasebook and Dictionary

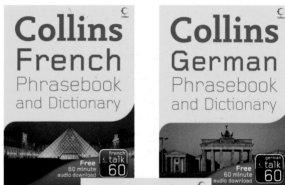

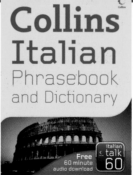

Other titles in the series
Greek Japanese Mandarin Polish Portuguese Spanish Turkish

Collins Easy: Photo Phrasebook

Also available as
**Phrasebook
CD Pack**

**Other titles
in the series**
Easy French
Easy Greek
Easy Italian

To order any of these titles, please telephone 0870 787 1732.
For further information about all Collins books, visit our website:
www.collins.co.uk